I0702978

Femme Fatale

and

Dark Feminine Energy

Secrets Revealed: Unleash Your Inner Femme Fatale and Become an Alpha Woman | Manifesting & Positive Affirmations Included

Written by **Victoria Garcia**

© Copyright 2024 - All rights reserved by Victoria Garcia

The content contained within this book may not be reproduced, duplicated or transmitted without direct written permission from the author or the publisher.

Under no circumstances will any blame or legal responsibility be held against the publisher, or author, for any damages, reparation, or monetary loss due to the information contained within this book, either directly or indirectly.

Legal Notice:
This book is copyright protected. It is only for personal use. You cannot amend, distribute, sell, use, quote or paraphrase any part, or the content within this book, without the consent of the author or publisher.

Disclaimer Notice:

The content provided in this book is offered for informational purposes only and reflects the current understanding and interpretations of the femme fatale archetype and its applications. The listener is advised that the application, use, or misuse of this information is at their own discretion and risk. Under no circumstances shall the author or the publisher be liable for any direct, indirect, incidental, or consequential damages or hardships arising from the use of the information contained in this book.

Furthermore, the information presented is intended solely for educational purposes and should not be considered exhaustive or universally applicable. It is presented with the understanding that the author and publisher are not engaged in rendering psychological, legal, or other professional services. If expert assistance is required, the services of a competent professional should be sought.

TABLE OF CONTENTS

Introduction - The Allure of The Femme Fatale

Congratulations on choosing this path of self-help and personal growth. Your decision to invest in yourself is commendable and will undoubtedly lead to a more empowered and fulfilling life. As you read through this book, remember that true understanding and transformation often require more than a single read. Taking the time to revisit chapters, reflect on the insights, and take detailed notes will deepen your comprehension and make the lessons more impactful.

In the following chapters, you will discover the multifaceted archetype of the femme fatale. From her historical and cultural significance to her portrayal in modern media, you will uncover the layers that make this figure both feared and revered. You will also explore the psychology behind her actions, learning how to apply similar traits in your own life with confidence and strategic foresight.

This book is designed to not only inform but to inspire action. By following the principles and techniques discussed, you will be able to redefine power, autonomy, and emotional intelligence within your own context. As you read, remember that growth is a continuous process. Revisit these concepts regularly, and don't hesitate to jot down thoughts and observations that resonate with you.

Thank you for choosing this book as your guide. May it serve as a valuable resource on your journey towards becoming a more confident, empowered version of yourself. Wishing you all the best as you start this exciting adventure.

Chapter 1 - Defining The Femme Fatale

The femme fatale is a powerful archetype symbolizing unapologetic strength and autonomy. She defies societal judgments and traditional narratives, pursuing her desires with relentless audacity. Her calculated and daring decisions reflect a profound understanding of her goals and the environments she maneuvers through. One of the most defining features of this figure is her profound grasp of human psychology. She sours through social landscapes with an acumen that allows her to anticipate and maneuver through various interpersonal dynamics. This emotional intelligence is not wielded as a mere tool for manipulation but as a strategic asset, helping her to achieve her ends while maintaining her autonomy.

She does not fit neatly into the roles traditionally assigned to women; instead, she questions and often overturns these roles. Her actions and choices can be seen as forms of rebellion against the constraints imposed on female behavior and expression. Through her, we explore themes of freedom, control, and the redefinition of power within a gendered context.

While traditionally viewed as manipulative and dangerous, a more nuanced view reveals her authenticity and vulnerability. These qualities are what make her relatable and real. Accepting vulnerability and turning it into a strength is a powerful message, and the femme fatale embodies this transformation, using her awareness of her strengths and weaknesses to forge a path that is uniquely hers.

Defining her thus involves recognizing her as a symbol of complex femininity—a figure that challenges us to reconsider our perceptions of power, autonomy, and emotional intelligence.

As we move forward to examine her historical and cultural significance and her portrayal in modern media, we will continue to uncover the layers that make her both a revered and feared figure in cultural narratives.

Historical and Cultural Significance of the Femme Fatale

The femme fatale, an archetype that transcends cultures and epochs, holds a mirror to society's evolving views on women and power. Her emergence in literature and art is not merely a reflection of male anxieties or fantasies but a complex response to the changing roles of women throughout history.

Understanding the historical and cultural significance offers us insights into the societal dynamics at play during various periods, showcasing how this figure has both been challenged and shaped by the norms of her time.

The origins of this archetype can be traced back to ancient mythologies where powerful female deities and figures such as Lilith, Medusa, and Circe, to name a few, played pivotal roles.

These figures were often depicted as both enchanting and dangerous, wielding their power over men and gods alike. This duality reflects early societal attempts to grapple with the concept of female autonomy and its implications.

In these stories, the femme fatale's power was intriguing yet threatening, a potent symbol of what could happen when women stepped outside the confines of societal expectations.

As we move into the Renaissance and later, the Victorian era, her portrayal shifts significantly. In these times, literature and art began to reflect more intensely the moral anxieties of society.
During these periods she is often depicted as a seductive, manipulative

woman who leads men to their doom. This portrayal is deeply entwined with the Victorian dichotomy of the "angel in the house" versus the "fallen woman," highlighting the era's strict moral codes and the consequences of their breach.

Characters like Carmen, Salome, and Lady Macbeth exemplify these traits, serving as cautionary tales against the dangers of unchecked female influence and sexuality.

With the advent of cinema, she found a new medium for expression, one that would cement her place in modern popular culture. The early 20th century, particularly the film noir era of the 1940s and 1950s, saw the femme fatale flourish.

Films like "Double Indemnity," "The Maltese Falcon," and "Gilda" featured charismatic and mysterious women who could manipulate their circumstances to get what they wanted, often at a high cost.

These characters were a response to post-war anxieties and the reassertion of traditional gender roles after women had experienced greater freedoms during the war years. The figure of a fatal woman in film noir could be seen as both a threat to the social order and a critique of the patriarchal society that sought to repress her.

In contemporary settings, this figure continues to evolve. Today, she might not only include the traditional seductress but also powerful businesswomen, politicians, or activists—women who challenge the status quo through their intellect and assertiveness.

Modern portrayals often seek to subvert the negative connotations associated with the femme fatale, presenting her as a figure of empowerment rather than a mere vessel of doom and destruction. This shift is reflective of broader societal changes toward gender perceptions and feminism, illustrating how the figure of the fatal woman has been reclaimed by women as a symbol of strength and independence.
As you may have understood, the historical and cultural significance of

this archetype is profound. By tracing her evolution, we gain a deeper understanding of the fears, desires, and tensions that have shaped gender dynamics across centuries.

I challenge you to see this evolution as an indication of the power of narrative in our lives—how stories not only reflect but can also reshape our realities.

The Femme Fatale in Modern Media

In today's media, femme fatales are not just the mysterious and dangerous women of classic film noir; they are complex characters who traverse through modern challenges, often embodying themes of empowerment, resistance, and identity.

Modern cinema and television, for example, have reimagined her, often blending her traditional characteristics with layers of depth and realism. In recent films and series, femme fatales can be seen as flawed, relatable individuals whose actions are grounded in personal motivations beyond mere seduction or manipulation.

For instance, characters in shows like "Killing Eve" or movies such as "Gone Girl" present a more psychological and intricate portrayal of this archetype, exploring their backgrounds, motivations, and the consequences of their actions in greater detail.

These characters are not defined solely by their relationships with men but are driven by a complex array of desires and ambitions, challenging viewers to empathize with them even as they enact morally ambiguous or outright villainous plans.

Literature and graphic novels have also contributed to this evolution, offering writers the space to scrutinize her psyche and environment with greater complexity.
In graphic novels, particularly, the visual element adds another layer of

expression, allowing for a more stylized and exaggerated exploration of the femme fatale. Works like "Sin City" or "Fatale" mix supernatural elements with noir aesthetics to create modern myths that reimagine the femme power and appeal in contexts that blur the lines between good and evil, real and fantastical.

Video games have emerged as a powerful medium for storytelling, with her taking center stage in narratives that explore themes ranging from redemption to revenge. In this interactive medium, players often encounter them as complex characters who can be allies, adversaries, or playable characters, such as in games like "Max Payne" and "Bayonetta." These characters provide gamers with an opportunity to explore the femme fatale's motivations and decisions firsthand, often affecting the outcome of the story based on their interactions with her.

Through her various incarnations, she challenges audiences to reconsider what it means to be a powerful woman in today's world. This ongoing dialogue highlights the shifting perceptions surrounding women who claim their power and defy traditional roles, reflecting broader debates about gender equality and representation.

All things considered, this figure remains vibrant and dynamic in modern media, constantly evolving to reflect the complexities of contemporary life and the shifting landscapes of power and gender.

By engaging with this archetype, creators and audiences alike participate in an ongoing discussion about the roles women play and the spaces they occupy in both the narrative and real worlds.

Chapter 2 - The Psychology of The Femme Fatale

This chapter explores the intriguing mindset and psychological traits of the femme fatale, an archetype that embodies strategic thinking, independence, and emotional intelligence. We will examine how her fearless approach to life's challenges, her mastery of self-presentation, and her unyielding determination define her character.

By understanding these psychological traits, we gain insights into her effectiveness in both fictional narratives and real-world scenarios. Through case studies from literature, film, and history, we will see how this complex figure operates and what she reveals about societal perceptions of powerful women.

Understanding Her Mindset

The mindset of the femme fatale is both intriguing and enlightening, a masterclass in steering through complex realities with strategic grace and unapologetic boldness. This archetype transcends mere seduction and manipulation, embodying a profound psychological complexity that illuminates the art of influence and self-determination.

At the core of the femme fatale's approach is her fearless nature, confronting life's complexities directly and viewing each obstacle as an opportunity to reaffirm her autonomy and advance her ambitions. Her actions are meticulously calculated, the result of strategic foresight and careful planning. She maneuvers through the present while always remaining several steps ahead, ensuring her decisions align with her long-term goals.

Her independence is not a mere preference but a fundamental aspect of her identity. She crafts her path with deliberate intention, relying on her capabilities and rarely seeking external validation. This self-sufficiency is empowering—it frees her from the constraints of traditional expectations and allows her to sail on her journey with authority and poise.

Also, her allure lies in her emotional intelligence. She adeptly reads and influences social dynamics, making her a formidable presence capable of handling complex interpersonal situations with ease.

The modern version of this figure often showcases a compelling blend of vulnerability and strength. This duality is not a contradiction but a confluence of traits that makes her deeply relatable and genuinely impactful. She strategically uses her vulnerability to connect and engage, drawing others closer and building relationships that serve both her emotional needs and practical purposes. Yet, her strength is never compromised; it is the core from which her resilience emanates. These traits are essential for anyone looking to go through their personal and professional lives with more confidence and effectiveness.

Psychological Traits Common to Femme Fatales

The femme fatale is a captivating archetype, rich with psychological complexity that transcends simple categorization. This chapter explores the core psychological traits that define her, traits that not only contribute to her mystique but also her effectiveness in various narratives and real-world analogues. These traits include a profound understanding of human nature, a mastery over self-presentation, and an unyielding determination to achieve personal goals.
A deep knowledge of the human psychology is one of her most distinctive traits. This is not merely academic knowledge but a profound, intuitive grasp of human desires, fears, and motivations. She uses this understanding to guide her social interactions expertly, manipulating circumstances to her advantage when necessary. This ability allows her to wield influence subtly yet effectively, making her a powerful player in any scenario.

She is acutely aware of the power of appearance and the perceptions of others. She masters the art of self-presentation, crafting her image and persona to fit the needs of the moment. Whether she chooses to appear vulnerable or commanding, her appearance is always a strategic decision, designed to elicit specific responses and achieve her aims. This skill in self-presentation is crucial, as it helps her control how she is perceived and, by extension, how much influence she can exert.

At her core, the femme fatale possesses an unyielding determination to achieve her objectives, regardless of the obstacles in her path. This tenacity is coupled with a remarkable resilience—an ability to rebound from setbacks without losing focus on her goals. These traits make her not only a survivor but a force to be reckoned with. She does not passively react to the world; instead, she actively shapes her environment to suit her needs.

The ability to adapt to changing circumstances is another key trait of the femme fatale. She is highly resourceful and capable of turning even unfavorable situations to her advantage. Her resourcefulness often surprises those around her, as she finds unconventional solutions to problems and hurdles.

While the she is often seen as manipulative, it's important to understand that her manipulative skills are grounded in high emotional intelligence. She can read emotional cues and respond in ways that advance her objectives, managing both her own emotions and those of others effectively. This emotional savvy provides her with a strategic advantage, enabling her to build the alliances and interactions necessary for her success.

As we move forward to explore case studies from fiction and reality, these traits will serve as a lens through which we can further analyze the impact and relevance of this archetype in both historical and contemporary contexts.

Case Studies from Fiction and Reality

The femme fatale archetype transcends fiction and reality, appearing in diverse contexts and stories. This section examine specific case studies, showcasing the enduring allure and complexity of the figure of this femme in literature, film, and historical figures. Through these examples, we gain deeper insights into how this archetype operates within narratives and what it unveils about societal perceptions of powerful women.

Fictional Representations

1. **Catherine Tramell from "Basic Instinct"**
   Catherine Tramell, the protagonist in the thriller "Basic Instinct," epitomizes the modern femme fatale. She is intelligent, charming, and sexually assertive, using her wit and allure to manipulate those around her while maintaining control over her narrative. Her character study provides insights into the femme fatale's ability to dominate the storyline and challenge the viewer's perceptions of morality and power.

2. **Lady Macbeth from Shakespeare's "Macbeth"**
   Although historical in setting, Lady Macbeth's role in Shakespeare's play offers a classic example of the femme fatale's influence in literature. Driven by ambition and power, she persuades Macbeth to commit regicide, exhibiting strong will, manipulation, and the dire consequences of unchecked ambition. Her psychological depth showcases the complex interplay of vulnerability and ruthlessness that often characterizes this archetype.

Real-Life Figures

1. **Mata Hari**
   Mata Hari, the infamous Dutch exotic dancer and courtesan

who was executed for espionage during World War I, is often considered a real-life femme fatale. Her life story, marked by accusations of double-dealing and manipulation, highlights how the femme fatale archetype can be projected onto women who challenge societal norms and wield their intelligence and sexuality in unconventional ways.

2. **Cleopatra VII**
    Cleopatra VII of Egypt, renowned for her political savvy and her romantic relationships with Julius Caesar and Mark Antony, is another historical figure often romanticized as a femme fatale. Her leadership and strategic marriages speak to her skills in political and emotional manipulation, illustrating the femme fatale's role in shaping history through personal and political influence.

Through these examples, we can appreciate the femme fatale's impact on narrative development and historical outcomes. Whether through the lens of literary critique or historical analysis, she remains a powerful symbol of the complexities of female empowerment and the societal responses it evokes. This exploration helps to demystify the archetype, showing that she can embody both a cautionary tale and a source of inspiration, reflecting broader themes of human behavior, power dynamics, and cultural expectations.

Chapter 3 - Crafting Your Femme Fatale Persona

In this chapter, we explore how to develop key traits associated with the femme fatale archetype, focusing on confidence, poise, and the art of mystery. We will discuss practical steps to build these qualities, such as setting achievable goals, engaging in positive self-talk, practicing mindfulness, seeking feedback, and role-playing challenging interactions. Additionally, we'll cover the strategic use of mystery and how to maintain a composed, consistent persona that keeps others intrigued. We'll also discuss the ethical use of manipulation tactics, emphasizing emotional intelligence and positive influence. By integrating these traits and strategies, you can improve your presence and effectiveness in both personal and professional settings.

Developing Confidence and Poise

The traits of confidence and poise are essential if you are seeking to handle life's challenges with grace and effectiveness. These qualities are especially prominent in the femme fatale archetype, symbolizing her control over her environment and her ability to influence others subtly. This chapter explores how one can develop these key traits, not only to boost personal interactions but to encourage a self-assured presence that commands respect and attention.

Confidence is not merely about self-assurance in one's abilities; it's about trust in one's capacity to handle whatever comes. It is a deep-seated belief that you can effectively manage the outcome of your actions, which in turn influences how you approach challenges and opportunities. For anyone looking to develop this trait, it starts with a foundation of self-awareness—recognizing your strengths and acknowledging areas for improvement without judgment.

Poise is closely linked to confidence but focuses more on demeanor and the ability to maintain composure in challenging situations. Developing poise requires mindfulness and control over one's emotions and reactions. It involves a calm, composed approach to life's surprises, allowing you to think clearly and act deliberately. Poise is especially useful in high-pressure environments where first impressions and quick decisions are crucial.

Practical Steps to Develop Confidence and Poise

1. SET ACHIEVABLE GOALS

Start with clear, achievable goals to gradually build your self-confidence. Achieving these goals will instill a sense of fulfillment and strengthen your confidence in your capabilities.

Here is how I usually set my goals:

Step 1: Define Your Goal

- **Identify what you want to achieve:** Be specific about what you want to accomplish. For example: "I want to develop confidence and poise in social and professional situations."

- **Write it down:** Writing your goal makes it tangible and helps you stay committed.

Step 2: Make Your Goal SMART

In order to do that, you have to consider this 5 points:

1. **Specific:** Clearly define what you want to achieve. Example: "I want to feel confident and poised when speaking in meetings and social gatherings."

2. **Measurable:** Establish criteria to measure progress and identify when the goal has been accomplished. Example: "I will track my progress by keeping a journal of my experiences and rating my confidence level from 1 to 10 after each situation."

3. **Achievable:** Ensure the goal is realistic and attainable, given

your current level of social skills

4. **Relevant:** Make sure the goal aligns with your broader objectives or values. Example: Developing confidence and poise is crucial for my personal growth and career advancement.

5. **Time-bound:** Set a deadline for achieving the goal.

Step 3: Break Down the Goal

- **Divide into smaller tasks:** Break the goal into smaller, manageable steps.

- **Set milestones:** Create checkpoints to monitor progress and stay motivated.

Step 4: Develop an Action Plan

- **List action steps:** Detail each task you need to complete to achieve the goal.

- **Prioritize tasks:** Determine the order in which tasks need to be completed.

- **Assign deadlines:** Set deadlines for each task to stay on track.

Step 5: Take Action

- **Start with the first task:** Begin working on your action plan immediately.

- **Stay consistent:** Regularly work on your tasks, even if progress seems slow.

Step 6: Monitor and Review Progress

- **Track your progress:** Use a journal, app, or planner to keep track of completed tasks and milestones.

- **Adjust as needed:** Be flexible and adjust your plan if you encounter obstacles or if things change.

The second step to achieve confident and poise is:

2.   ENGAGE IN POSITIVE SELF-TALK

The way you talk to yourself influences your mindset significantly. Engage in positive self-talk to reinforce your self-worth and combat negative thoughts. This practice will help solidify your internal foundation of confidence.

Strategies to Improve Positive Self-Talk
1. Awareness and Recognition

- **Identify Negative Thoughts:** Pay attention to your inner dialogue and recognize when you're being self-critical.

- **Journal:** Keep a journal to record your thoughts and feelings. This helps in identifying patterns of negative self-talk.

2. Challenge Negative Thoughts

- **Question the Validity:** Ask yourself if the negative thought is based on facts or assumptions. Challenge its validity.

- **Reframe:** Replace negative thoughts with positive or neutral ones. Instead of "I can't do this," say "I can try my best."

3. Affirmations

- **Create Positive Statements:** Develop affirmations that reflect your goals and strengths. Repeat them daily.

- **Be Specific:** Make your affirmations specific and believable. Instead of "I am successful," say "I am capable of achieving my goals."

4. Visualization

- **Positive Visualization:** Visualize yourself succeeding in various situations. Imagine the positive feelings associated with success.

- **Practice Daily:** Spend a few minutes each day visualizing positive outcomes.

5. Self-Compassion

- **Be Kind to Yourself:** Show yourself the same kindness and understanding that you would extend to a friend.

- **Forgive Mistakes:** Understand that everyone makes mistakes. Learn from them instead of dwelling on them.

6. Surround Yourself with Positivity

- **Positive Environment:** Surround yourself with supportive and positive people.

- **Consume Positive Content:** Read books, listen to podcasts, and watch videos that inspire and uplift you.

Examples of Positive Self-Talk

Before a Presentation

- **Negative Thought:** "I'm going to mess up and everyone will think I'm incompetent."

- **Positive Reframe:** "I've prepared well for this presentation. I'll do my best and it will be a valuable experience."

When Facing a Challenge

- **Negative Thought:** "This is too hard. I can't do it."

- Positive Reframe: "This is a challenge, but I am capable of finding a solution and learning from this experience."

After Making a Mistake

- **Negative Thought:** "I always mess up. I'm so bad at this."

- **Positive Reframe:** "Everyone makes mistakes. I will learn from this and improve next time."

General Confidence Building

- **Negative Thought:** "I'm not good enough."

- **Positive Reframe:** "I am constantly growing and improving. I am proud of my progress."

Daily Affirmations

- "I am capable and strong."

- "I trust myself to make good decisions."

- "I am deserving of success and happiness."

- "I believe in my abilities and express my true self with confidence."

Implement this daily and you will start to notice an exponential increase in your positive self-talk immediately.

3. **Practice Mindfulness and Emotional Regulation** Developing poise involves regulating your emotions effectively. Practices like meditation, deep breathing exercises, and mindfulness can help you maintain calmness and balance in stressful situations.

One of my favorite exercises, which I consider to be one of the most effective, is a breathing exercise. It's very simple but effective. You just need to follow these steps:

Steps:

1. **Find a Quiet Space:**

    o Sit or lie down in a comfortable position in a quiet place where you won't be disturbed.

2. **Get Comfortable:**

    o Close your eyes and relax your body. Let your shoulders drop and your hands rest comfortably.

3. **Focus on Your Breath:**

   o   Bring your attention to your breath. Notice the sensation of the air entering and leaving your nostrils or the rise and fall of your chest.

4. **Deep Breaths:**

   o   Take a slow, deep breath in through your nose for a count of four.

   o   Hold the breath for a count of four.

   o   Exhale slowly through your mouth for a count of six.

   o   Pause briefly before taking another breath.

5. **Stay Present:**

   o   Continue to breathe deeply and slowly, maintaining your focus on the sensation of your breath.

   o   If your mind starts to wander, gently bring your focus back to your breath without judgment.

6. **Duration:**

   o   Practice this breathing exercise for 5-10 minutes. Set a timer if needed.

Benefits:

- **Reduces Stress:** Calms the nervous system and reduces the physical symptoms of stress.

- **Increases Focus:** Helps you stay present and improves concentration.

- **Promotes Relaxation:** Eases tension in the body and mind, leading to a state of relaxation.

Example Use:

When you feel overwhelmed at work or in any stressful situation, take a few minutes to practice mindful breathing. This simple exercise can help you regain composure, reduce anxiety, and approach tasks with a clearer, calmer mind.

By incorporating mindful breathing into your daily routine, you can effectively regulate your emotions and maintain a sense of calm throughout your day.

4.   SEEK FEEDBACK AND LEARN CONTINUOUSLY

Embrace feedback as a tool for growth. Learning from both successes and failures builds resilience and confidence, while continuous learning keeps you prepared and informed, enhancing your poise in various situations.

5.   ROLE PLAY CHALLENGING INTERACTIONS

Simulating challenging social or professional interactions can prepare you for real-life scenarios. This practice helps you develop and maintain poise by allowing you to experiment with different approaches in a controlled environment.

Developing confidence and poise is not an overnight process but a journey of self-discovery and improvement. By setting realistic goals, engaging in positive self-dialogue, practicing emotional control, seeking constructive feedback, and preparing for challenging situations, you can develop these qualities effectively. These traits not only enhance how you perceive yourself but also influence how others perceive you, paving the way for more meaningful and impactful interactions in both personal and professional settings.

Mastering the Art of Mystery

The art of mystery is a powerful tool in personal and professional interactions, enhancing allure and intrigue while maintaining a sense of depth that invites others to learn more. The femme fatale archetype masterfully uses mystery not just as a shield but as a strategic asset, balancing disclosure and secrecy to captivate and influence. This chapter explores how to grow and utilize mystery in your own life to enhance your presence and effectiveness in various situations.

Mystery serves multiple functions; it creates curiosity, commands attention, and can lead others to perceive you as more interesting and desirable. By carefully managing what you reveal about yourself, you encourage others to invest more effort into understanding you, which can increase your perceived value and authority.

Strategies to Develop Mystery

1.   BE SELECTIVE IN SHARING INFORMATION

The essence of mystery lies in selectivity. Share enough to pique interest but hold back enough to encourage further inquiry. This doesn't mean being secretive for the sake of it but rather sharing information thoughtfully to maintain engagement and interest.

Here is a real-life example:

Scenario: First Date at a Café

Imagine you're on a first date with someone you've recently met. You want to leave a memorable impression and make them interested in seeing you again.

Interaction Example:

You: "Hi, I'm Emily. I work in tech innovation, specifically focusing on cutting-edge solutions in data security."

Date: "Nice to meet you, Emily! Data security sounds fascinating. What kind of projects are you working on right now?"

You: "I'm currently involved in a really exciting project that's pushing the boundaries of AI in cybersecurity. It's something I'm passionate about, but I can't share too many details just yet. Let's just say it has the potential to revolutionize how we approach data protection."

Date: "Wow, that sounds intriguing! I'd love to hear more about it when you can share. How did you get into this field?"

You: "It's been quite a journey. I started in software development and gradually shifted towards cybersecurity after realizing the increasing importance of data protection. It's been an amazing ride, and there are so many layers to it. But enough about work. What about you? What do you enjoy doing in your free time?"

Breakdown of Selective Sharing

1. **Introduce Yourself Briefly:**

   o   You provide a concise and interesting introduction about your field without diving into all the details.

2. **Pique Interest with a Tease:**

   o   You mention your involvement in an exciting project but deliberately withhold specific details, sparking curiosity.

3. **Shift the Focus:**

   o   You engage the other person by asking about their interests, making the conversation two-sided and keeping the mystery about your work alive.

Outcome

By sharing selectively, you achieve several things:

- **Maintain Engagement:** Your date remains curious and interested in learning more about your work and background.

- **Create a Memorable Impression:** The intrigue surrounding your project and career makes you stand out in their memory.

- **Encourage Future Interactions:** By not revealing everything at once, you leave room for follow-up conversations, which can help build a stronger connection over time.

2.   SPEAK LESS, LISTEN MORE

Listening more than you speak is a powerful strategy. It not only makes you appear more thoughtful and discerning but also gives you insights into the motivations and personalities of others, which you can use to your advantage.

For instance, continuing with the example mentioned before:

Date: "I really enjoy hiking and exploring new trails. Being out in nature helps me relax and unwind after a busy week."

You: "That sounds wonderful. Do you have a favorite trail or place you like to hike?"

Date: "Yes, there's this beautiful trail near the mountains that I absolutely love. It's challenging but the view at the top is totally worth it."

You: "That's amazing. What do you enjoy most about hiking?"

Date: "Well, it's not just the scenery, but also the sense of accomplishment I feel when I reach the top. Plus, it's a great workout!"

You: "I can imagine. It must be really rewarding to reach the top and take in that view."

Date: "Absolutely. Have you ever tried hiking?"

You: "I have, but probably not as extensively as you. What got you into hiking in the first place?"

Date: "I've always loved being outdoors, but I got more into hiking in the last few years. It's become a big part of my routine."

You: "It's great that you have something so fulfilling in your life. Do you usually hike alone or with friends?"

Date: "I mix it up. Sometimes I enjoy the solitude, and other times I go with friends. It's nice to share the experience with someone."

You: "That sounds like a good balance. What's one of your most memorable hiking experiences?"

Date: "There was this one time when we got caught in a rainstorm on the way back down. It was challenging, but we made it through and it was such a bonding experience with my friends."

You: "Wow, that sounds intense! It's great that you turned it into a positive experience."

Breakdown of Speaking Less, Listening More

1. **Ask Open-Ended Questions:**

    o You ask questions that encourage your date to share more about their interests and experiences.

2. **Show Genuine Interest:**

    o You actively listen and show genuine curiosity about what your date enjoys.

3. **Encourage Them to Elaborate:**

    o You prompt them to go into more detail, which makes them feel valued and understood.

4. **Reflect and Affirm:**

    o You reflect back what they've shared and affirm their feelings and experiences.

Outcome

By speaking less and listening more, you achieve several things:

- **Build a Connection:** Your date feels heard and valued, which helps build a deeper connection.

- **Gain Insights:** You learn more about your date's motivations, interests, and personality.

- **Appear Thoughtful:** You come across as a thoughtful and discerning person, making a positive impression.

3. KEEP YOUR CALM

A calm and composed demeanor contributes significantly to an aura of mystery. Avoid oversharing personal emotions or reactions publicly. Displaying a controlled response, especially in unexpected situations, can enhance your mysterious aura.

Let's say that while we are continuing our acquaintance, the person in question makes a rude comment. Instead of reacting angrily and emotionally, this could be a viable alternative:

Date: "By the way, I'm not really into short hair. I prefer women with longer hair."

You (remaining calm and composed): "I see. Well, I guess it's a good thing I'm not a hair model then! So, back to your hiking adventures—what's another trail you'd recommend?"

An exercise that has helped me greatly in developing calmness even in situations where negative emotions might prevail is visualization:

Visualize yourself handling unexpected comments with grace and composure. This mental rehearsal can prepare you to respond calmly in real life.

Remind yourself that most comments are reflections of the other person's preferences and not a judgment of your worth. Be aware of your initial emotional responses and choose to respond thoughtfully rather than react impulsively. Practice pausing before speaking or acting.

4. MAINTAIN A CONSISTENT PERSONA

Consistency in your behavior and presentation reinforces the mystique. If people can predict your reactions or thoughts easily, the sense of mystery is lost. Keeping a consistent but slightly unpredictable persona makes others keen to know more about your thoughts and actions.

Advice: To maintain a consistent persona, blend predictability with subtle unpredictability. This means being reliable in your core values and behaviors while occasionally surprising your date with new and intriguing aspects of yourself.

How to Do This

1. **Core Consistency:**

   o **Stay True to Your Values:** Your fundamental values and principles should always shine through. If you value honesty, kindness, or intellectual curiosity, these traits should consistently be part of your interactions.

   o **Reliable Behavior:** Be dependable in your actions. If you say you'll do something, follow through.

2. **Subtle Unpredictability:**

   o **Introduce New Topics:** Occasionally bring up a new topic or share an interest they didn't know about. For example, if they think they know your hobbies, mention an unexpected but genuine interest, like "By the way, I also enjoy painting. It's a relaxing way to express myself."

   o **Spontaneous Plans:** Suggest spontaneous activities or date ideas. If your dates have been casual coffee meetings, propose an impromptu visit to an art exhibit or a new hiking trail you found interesting.

Let's look at an example still related to the previous situation:"

You: "It's great that you have something so fulfilling in your life. Do you usually hike alone or with friends?"

Date: "I mix it up. Sometimes I enjoy the solitude, and other times I go with friends. It's nice to share the experience with someone."

You: "That sounds like a good balance. Speaking of balance, I've also found something new that's been really rewarding for me – pottery. It's a fantastic way to unwind and be creative. Have you ever tried it?"

Date: "No, I haven't! That sounds interesting. How did you get into pottery?"

You: "I stumbled upon a workshop a few months ago and decided to give it a try. Now, it's something I look forward to every week. If you're ever interested, we could check out a class together sometime."

Outcome

By maintaining a consistent persona with elements of subtle unpredictability:

- **Build Trust:** Your date will see you as reliable and trustworthy because of your consistent core values.

- **Keep Interest Alive:** The slight unpredictability keeps things exciting and makes them keen to know more about you.

- **Strengthen Connection:** Balancing reliability with intriguing new aspects helps build a deeper, more dynamic connection.

5.   DEVELOP UNIQUE INTERESTS AND SKILLS

Referring back to point number 4, Having unique hobbies or skills that others find intriguing can add layers to your mystique. These pursuits give others a glimpse into your world, increasing their curiosity about your other, less visible traits.

If you are a curious person who likes to experiment, these are some excellent activities, interests, or skills to try or acquire.

Creative Pursuits

1. **Pottery and Ceramics:** Working with clay is both therapeutic and creative, producing beautiful, tangible results.

2. **Painting or Drawing:** Expressing yourself through art can be both relaxing and a way to showcase your creativity.

3. **Photography:** Capturing moments and telling stories through images can be a captivating skill.

4. **Writing:** Whether it's poetry, short stories, or journaling, writing can be a powerful form of self-expression.

5. **Music:** Playing an instrument or composing music can be incredibly engaging and impressive.

Intellectual Activities

6. **Chess:** This classic game sharpens your strategic thinking and is often seen as a mark of intelligence.

7. **Philosophy:** Engaging with philosophical texts and discussions can provide profound insights and spark interesting conversations.

8. **Foreign Languages:** Learning new languages opens up cultural doors and enhances communication skills.

9. **Cryptography:** The study of codes and encryption is a fascinating and highly specialized field.

10. **Astrophysics or Astronomy:** Understanding the universe can be both humbling and intellectually stimulating.

Physical Activities

11. **Rock Climbing:** This sport combines physical strength with problem-solving skills and offers a sense of adventure.

12. **Martial Arts:** Practicing disciplines like karate, judo, or taekwondo can enhance physical fitness and self-discipline.

13. **Sailing:** Navigating the waters can be thrilling and teaches patience and resilience.

14. **Yoga:** This practice promotes physical health, mental well-being, and inner peace.

15. **Fencing:** This elegant sport combines physical agility with strategic thinking.

Cultural and Social Activities

16. **Wine Tasting:** Understanding the nuances of different wines can be both a sophisticated and enjoyable hobby.

17. **Travel Blogging:** Sharing your travel experiences and insights can inspire others and showcase your adventurous side.

18. **Historical Reenactment:** Participating in historical reenactments can be a unique and educational way to engage with history.

19. **Theater Acting:** Performing in theater can enhance your confidence and public speaking skills.

20. **Volunteering:** Engaging in community service can highlight your compassion and commitment to social causes.

Technological Skills

21. **Robotics:** Building and programming robots can be a cutting-edge and intellectually stimulating hobby.

22. **3D Printing:** Creating objects with 3D printing technology can be both fun and innovative.

23. **Coding and App Development:** Developing software or apps can be a highly valued and creative skill.

24. **Drone Piloting:** Flying drones and capturing aerial footage is both exciting and technologically advanced.

25. **Virtual Reality Design:** Creating VR experiences combines creativity with technology.

In conclusion, even an effective use of silence and timing can greatly enhance the aura of mystery. Knowing when to pause in conversation, when to respond, and when to leave something unsaid can make your communications more impactful. The strategic use of silence invites others to fill the gap, often revealing more about themselves than they realize.

Mastering the art of mystery is not about deception or avoidance but about strategic self-presentation and communication. By being selective in sharing information, enhancing listening skills, maintaining composure, being consistent in your persona, and developing unique interests, you can develop a magnetic presence that draws people in.

The skills developed through mastering mystery will prove invaluable, allowing for more nuanced and effective interactions in both personal and professional realms.

Emotional Intelligence and Manipulation Tactics

Are you familiar with the concept of emotional intelligence? It emerged in the 1990s from the research of psychologist and writer Daniel Goleman. Emotional intelligence is a type of intelligence that is different from the "traditional" kind because it involves empathizing with the emotional states of others. It focuses on recognizing, understanding, and managing both your own emotions and those of others. The ability to connect deeply with emotions is essential for building strong interpersonal relationships, making effective decisions (in both work and personal life), and dealing with daily challenges with awareness. Emotional intelligence is a valuable tool for improving your life and personal growth, as it allows you to comprehend the emotional complexity of yourself and those around you and respond appropriately to various situations.

What are the key components of emotional intelligence?

As mentioned earlier, the term "emotional intelligence" was introduced by psychologist and writer Daniel Goleman. It refers to the ability to recognize, understand, and express your own and others' emotions, as well as manage them effectively to achieve personal and relational goals more easily. In an interview with Forbes, Goleman states that "The ability to manage oneself, be self-aware, and self-regulate, is the foundation for learning to manage others (...)". Daniel Goleman identifies five key components of emotional intelligence:

1. Self-awareness: the ability to recognize your own emotions and feelings, understand the impact they have on your actions and behavior, and identify both your strengths and emotional weaknesses.

2. Self-regulation and emotional control: the ability to guide and control your own emotions and impulsive reactions, adapt to changes, and stay calm even in stressful situations.

3. Motivation: having the emotional drive to achieve your goals and the persistence to overcome difficulties, using your inner resources.

4. Empathy: empathy and emotional intelligence are closely linked. Empathy is the ability to understand and share the feelings of others. Being empathetic allows you to build deep, meaningful, and fulfilling relationships and improve

interpersonal communication.

5. Social skills: the ability to interact effectively with others, manage conflicts, and build positive interpersonal relationships.

However, not everyone possesses a well-developed emotional intelligence. Let's look at what happens when someone has low emotional intelligence and how it can be improved.

What happens if you have low emotional intelligence? If someone has low emotional intelligence, they might find it difficult to manage their own emotions and understand the feelings of others. This can lead to communication issues, relationship problems, impulse control challenges (such as managing anger), and difficulties in handling stress. On the other hand, people with high emotional intelligence tend to have more fulfilling and rewarding lives. They are more likely to build strong and enriching relationships, handle their emotions and complex feelings better, have higher self-esteem, and achieve their goals more effectively.

What benefits does emotional intelligence provide? Emotional intelligence can enhance romantic relationships by helping you understand and manage your own emotions and those of your partner, leading to effective communication and a deeper connection. Professionally, emotional intelligence can also be very beneficial. An "emotional leader" can recognize and deeply understand their own emotions and those of their team members, using this understanding constructively to be an inspiring guide. If you're interested in this topic, this article explains how to become a successful leader.

Is emotional intelligence innate, or can it be developed and improved over time? Emotional intelligence can be developed and improved over time with some straightforward practices. Creating positive habits can lead to well-being and inner growth, resulting in great satisfaction and fulfillment. Here are 8 strategies to develop emotional intelligence:

1. Practice self-reflection: set aside time daily to reflect on your

emotions, behaviors, and reactions.

2. Develop self-awareness: pay attention to your emotional states and reactions in different situations.

3. Active listening and empathy: understanding the emotions and perspectives of others is important for responding appropriately, building meaningful conversations, and establishing relationships of trust and respect.

4. Stress management: learning relaxation, breathing, or meditation techniques can help you handle stressful situations more calmly.

5. Effective communication: improve your ability to express your emotions and needs clearly and assertively to avoid ambiguity or misunderstandings.

6. Practice gratitude: recognize the positive things in life and be thankful for every little opportunity each day.

7. Be open to change: learn from experiences and adapt to new situations. This will help you face challenges with less fear and more enthusiasm.

8. Develop social skills: actively participate in social situations, enrich dialogue, practice active listening, and improve understanding of others.

These habits and practices can be developed daily by anyone. Growing and improving is part of the process of inner change. Developing emotional intelligence leads to greater self-awareness and understanding of others, with noticeable benefits in all areas of life.

Ethical Manipulation Tactics

While manipulation generally carries a negative connotation, when framed as strategic influence and used ethically, it can lead to mutually beneficial outcomes. The key is ensuring that these tactics respect the autonomy and dignity of all involved:

1. FRAMING COMMUNICATION STRATEGICALLY

Framing communication strategically involves presenting ideas and messages in ways that resonate with others' values and emotions, making them more receptive to your viewpoint.

This approach can significantly enhance the effectiveness of your communication by ensuring that your message aligns with the listener's perspectives, beliefs, and emotional state. By doing so, you create a connection that makes your ideas more compelling and acceptable to others.

Strategic framing is particularly useful in various scenarios, including professional settings, personal relationships, and social interactions. It requires a deep understanding of the audience and the ability to tailor your communication to meet their needs and preferences. This involves not only what you say but also how you say it, considering the tone, context, and delivery of your message.

Key Components of Strategic Framing

1. **Understanding who you are dealing with:**

    o **Values:** What is important to them? What do they care about?

    o **Emotions:** What are their current emotional states? What emotions might your message evoke?

    o **Beliefs and Attitudes:** What are their existing beliefs and attitudes towards the topic?

2. **Crafting the Message:**

    o **Relevance:** Make sure your message is relevant to the audience's interests and concerns.

- o **Clarity:** Use clear and straightforward language that is easy to understand.

- o **Appeal to Emotions:** Use emotional appeals where appropriate to create a stronger connection.

3. **Delivery:**

    - o **Tone and Style:** Adjust your tone and style to match the audience's preferences.

    - o **Timing:** Choose the right moment to deliver your message for maximum impact.

    - o **Medium:** Select the appropriate medium (face-to-face, email, presentation) for your message.

Real-Life Examples
Example 1: Professional Setting

Scenario: You are a project manager trying to convince the senior management team to invest in a new software tool that will improve team productivity.

Strategic Framing:

- **Understanding the Audience:** Senior management values efficiency, cost-effectiveness, and return on investment (ROI).

- **Crafting the Message:**

    - o **Relevance:** "This new software tool addresses our current bottlenecks in project management and can streamline our processes."

    - o **Clarity:** "It integrates with our existing systems and has a user-friendly interface."

    - o **Appeal to Emotions:** "By adopting this tool, we can

reduce employee stress and increase job satisfaction, leading to higher productivity and lower turnover."

- **Delivery:**

  - **Tone and Style:** Professional and confident.

  - **Timing:** Present the proposal during a scheduled meeting for budget discussions.

  - **Medium:** Use a presentation with visuals showing the benefits and potential ROI.

Example Pitch: "Implementing this software tool will streamline our project management processes, saving each team member approximately 2 hours per week. This efficiency gain translates into a 15% increase in productivity, ultimately enhancing our bottom line. Moreover, the tool's user-friendly interface will reduce employee stress and improve job satisfaction, supporting a more motivated and committed workforce."

Example 2: Personal Relationship

Scenario: You want to persuade your partner to adopt a healthier lifestyle together.

Strategic Framing:

- **Understanding the Audience:** Your partner values quality time together and has expressed interest in improving health.

- **Crafting the Message:**

  - **Relevance:** "We've both talked about wanting to feel better and have more energy."

  - **Clarity:** "Starting a routine like jogging or cooking healthy meals together can be a fun and effective way to achieve this."

- o **Appeal to Emotions:** "Imagine how much more enjoyable our weekends could be if we're both feeling our best and spending time doing healthy activities together."

- **Delivery:**

  - o **Tone and Style:** Warm and supportive.

  - o **Timing:** During a relaxed moment, such as a quiet evening at home.

  - o **Medium:** Face-to-face conversation.

Example Pitch: "I've been thinking about how we both want to have more energy and feel healthier. What if we started jogging together in the mornings or tried cooking new healthy recipes in the evenings? It could be a fun way to spend more time together, and we'll feel so much better for it. Plus, we could support each other and make it a shared goal."

Example 3: Social Interaction

Scenario: You're part of a community group and want to propose a new initiative to clean up local parks.

Strategic Framing:

- **Understanding the Audience:** Community members value the environment, safety, and local engagement.

- **Crafting the Message:**

  - o **Relevance:** "Keeping our parks clean will provide a safer and more enjoyable environment for everyone."

  - o **Clarity:** "We can organize monthly clean-up events where volunteers gather to pick up litter and maintain the park."

- o **Appeal to Emotions:** "By participating, we not only improve our local parks but also build a stronger, more connected community."

- **Delivery:**

  - o **Tone and Style:** Enthusiastic and inclusive.

  - o **Timing:** At a community meeting or through a community newsletter.

  - o **Medium:** Face-to-face announcement or written proposal.

Example Pitch: "Imagine our local parks as clean, safe spaces where our children can play and we can all enjoy nature. I propose we start a monthly clean-up event. It's a great way to take care of our environment and bring our community closer together. We can make a real difference, and it'll be a fun and rewarding activity for everyone involved."

Framing communication strategically is a powerful way to ensure your messages resonate with others' values and emotions, making them more receptive to your viewpoint. By understanding your audience, crafting relevant and clear messages, and delivering them effectively, you can significantly enhance the impact of your communication in various aspects of life.

2. CREATING POSITIVE ASSOCIATIONS

Creating positive associations can subtly influence how people feel about you and your ideas by linking your proposals with positive emotions, contexts, or outcomes. This psychological technique leverages the power of association to build favorable perceptions and strengthen your influence. By associating your ideas, actions, or presence with positive experiences and emotions, you make it more likely that others will view you and your proposals in a positive light.

Positive associations can be created through various methods, such as highlighting the benefits of your ideas, using uplifting and encouraging language, or aligning your proposals with widely valued outcomes. This approach is particularly effective in both personal and professional interactions, as it helps to build rapport, trust, and a sense of shared purpose.

Key Components of Creating Positive Associations

1. **Highlight Benefits:**

   o **Showcase Positive Outcomes:** Emphasize the positive results that will come from adopting your ideas or proposals.

   o **Use Real-Life Examples:** Share success stories or testimonials that illustrate the benefits.

2. **Use Uplifting Language:**

   o **Encouraging Words:** Use language that is motivating and positive.

   o **Positive Tone:** Maintain an optimistic and enthusiastic tone in your communication.

3. **Align with Values:**

   o **Shared Values:** Connect your ideas to the values and priorities of your audience.

   o **Common Goals:** Highlight how your proposals align with common goals or interests.

4. **Create Positive Experiences:**

   o **Engaging Interactions:** Ensure that interactions are pleasant and engaging.

   o **Supportive Environment:** Foster an environment that

supports and encourages positive emotions.

Example of Creating Positive Associations in Early Relationships

Scenario: Early Stages of a Romantic Relationship

You've just started dating someone, and you want to create positive associations to deepen the connection and make them feel good about spending time with you.

Creating Positive Associations

Creating Positive Associations: Focus on highlighting the enjoyable and memorable experiences you can share together, use uplifting and encouraging language, and align activities with shared interests and values.

Interaction Example

You and your date are planning your next outing.

You: "I've been thinking about what we could do for our next date. How about we try that new outdoor movie theater in the park? It's such a unique experience, and I heard they're showing a classic film this weekend."

Date: "That sounds like a lot of fun! I've never been to an outdoor movie theater before."

You: "I think you'll love it. There's something magical about watching a movie under the stars. Plus, we can bring a picnic, relax on a blanket, and just enjoy each other's company. It'll be a perfect blend of fun and relaxation."

Date: "I really like that idea. It sounds so different from the usual dates."

You: "Great! I'm excited for it too. I'll take care of the picnic—what kind of snacks do you enjoy? I want to make sure it's something you'll love."

Date: "I'm a fan of cheese and crackers, and maybe some fresh fruit."

You: "Perfect! I'll bring those and maybe a little surprise treat as well. I'm looking forward to making it a special night for us."

Breakdown of Positive Associations

1. **Highlight Benefits:**

    o **Enjoyable Experience:** Emphasize the unique and enjoyable aspects of the outdoor movie theater.

    o **Relaxation and Fun:** Highlight the blend of relaxation and fun that the experience offers.

2. **Use Uplifting Language:**

    o **Positive Tone:** Use enthusiastic and positive language to describe the activity.

    o **Encouraging Words:** Show excitement and encouragement for the shared experience.

3. **Align with Values:**

    o **Shared Interests:** Choose an activity that aligns with both your interests, such as enjoying movies and spending time outdoors.

    o **Personal Touch:** Tailor the experience by considering your date's preferences, like their favorite snacks.

4. **Create Positive Experiences:**

    o **Memorable Outing:** Plan an outing that is likely to create lasting positive memories.

o **Thoughtful Gestures:** Include thoughtful touches, like preparing a picnic with your date's favorite snacks.

By planning an enjoyable and unique date, using uplifting language, and incorporating your date's preferences, you create positive associations with spending time together. This helps deepen the connection and makes your date look forward to future outings, associating you with enjoyable and memorable experiences.

3. UTILIZING THE PRINCIPLE OF RECIPROCITY by doing favors or offering help without immediate expectation of return can encourage others to feel inclined to support you when you need it.

Utilizing the Principle of Reciprocity in Friendships

Utilizing the principle of reciprocity involves doing favors or offering help without immediate expectation of return, which can encourage others to feel inclined to support you when you need it. This principle is rooted in the idea that humans are naturally inclined to return favors, creating a cycle of mutual support and cooperation. By helping others generously and selflessly, you build a network of goodwill that can provide support when you face challenges or need assistance.

In the context of friendships, the principle of reciprocity can strengthen bonds, build trust, and create a sense of community and belonging. When friends see that you are willing to go out of your way to help them, they are more likely to feel valued and appreciated, which in turn motivates them to reciprocate your kindness.

Key Components of Utilizing Reciprocity

1. **Genuine Help:**

   o Offer help sincerely without expecting anything in return. Genuine acts of kindness build stronger, more authentic relationships.

2. **Timeliness:**

   o   Offer assistance when it's most needed. Timely help is often more impactful and appreciated.

3. **Consistency:**

   o   Regularly engage in acts of kindness. Consistent behavior reinforces the perception of reliability and trustworthiness.

4. **Empathy:**

   o   Understand the needs and challenges of your friends. Offering help that is truly beneficial to them shows empathy and thoughtfulness.

Real-Life Examples in Friendships
Example 1: Offering Support During Stressful Times

Scenario: Your friend is going through a particularly stressful period at work and is struggling to manage their time.

Utilizing Reciprocity:

- **Genuine Help:** Offer to assist with tasks or provide emotional support without expecting anything in return.

- **Timeliness:** Provide your support during their peak stress times to make a significant impact.

- **Consistency:** Check in regularly to see how they're doing and offer continuous support.

4. APPEALING TO PEOPLE'S SELF-CONCEPT

Appealing to people's self-concept involves aligning your objectives with how individuals see themselves or aspire to be, thus motivating them to act in ways that reinforce their self-image. The self-concept is a powerful driver of human behavior, encompassing our beliefs, values, and aspirations. When communication is framed to resonate with a person's self-concept, it taps into their intrinsic motivations, making them more likely to respond positively and take desired actions.

This strategy is particularly effective because people naturally seek consistency between their actions and their self-perception. By aligning your message with their self-concept, you make it easier for them to see how supporting your ideas or initiatives also supports their identity and values.

Key Components of Appealing to Self-Concept

1. **Understanding Self-Concept:**

   o **Current Self-Concept:** How do individuals currently see themselves? What are their core values and beliefs?

   o **Aspirational Self-Concept:** How do they aspire to be? What qualities or achievements do they strive for?

2. **Crafting the Message:**

   o **Alignment:** Ensure your message aligns with their self-perception or aspirations.

   o **Reinforcement:** Highlight how supporting your objective reinforces their self-image.

   o **Empowerment:** Empower them to see the positive impact of their actions on their identity.

3. **Delivery:**

   o **Personalization:** Tailor the message to resonate personally with the individual or group.

   o **Authenticity:** Communicate genuinely and authentically to build trust and connection.

o   **Encouragement:** Encourage them to take action by emphasizing the alignment with their self-concept.

Real-Life Examples
Example 1: Professional Setting

Scenario: You are a team leader trying to motivate your team to adopt a new workflow system.

Appealing to Self-Concept:

- **Understanding Self-Concept:** Your team sees themselves as innovative, efficient, and committed to excellence.

- **Crafting the Message:**

    o   **Alignment:** "This new workflow system is designed to enhance our innovation and efficiency, which are key strengths of our team."

    o   **Reinforcement:** "By adopting this system, we can continue to set the standard for excellence in our field."

    o   **Empowerment:** "Implementing this change will showcase our ability to adapt and lead in the industry."

Example Pitch: "As a team that prides itself on being innovative and efficient, adopting this new workflow system is a natural step forward. It's specifically designed to streamline our processes and enhance our productivity, aligning perfectly with our commitment to excellence. By leading this change, we reinforce our reputation as trailblazers in the industry and continue to set the benchmark for others."

The application of emotional intelligence and manipulation tactics requires a delicate balance to ensure that influence does not become coercion. It is crucial to respect others' feelings and autonomy, aiming for outcomes that enhance connection and mutual benefit. Transparency about intentions and maintaining integrity in your interactions are vital to keeping these tactics within ethical boundaries.

Developing emotional intelligence and understanding ethical manipulation tactics are crucial for anyone looking to enhance their interpersonal effectiveness and leadership abilities. These skills allow people to handle complex social landscapes with greater ease and effectiveness, promoting environments where motivation and commitment develop naturally. As we integrate these principles, we become more adept at leading, influencing, and connecting with others in deeply meaningful ways. This not only benefits our personal and professional growth but also contributes to a more emotionally intelligent and responsive society.

Chapter 4 - Style and Appearance

The fashion of the femme fatale is iconic, embodying a blend of sophistication, mystery, and undeniable allure. Her style is not just about appearance; it's a critical component of her identity, reflecting her confidence, control, and sensuality. This chapter explores the key fashion essentials that define the femme fatale's iconic look, empowering any woman to channel this confidence in her personal style.

We'll examine how the right colors, cuts, and fabrics can create a powerful presence. Discover the importance of makeup and hairstyling in enhancing mystique and elegance. Learn the art of accessorizing, from statement jewelry to practical handbags, and understand how each piece contributes to a captivating appearance. This chapter will provide practical tips to help you embrace the essence of the femme fatale in your everyday style, boosting your confidence and asserting your presence.

Fashion Essentials for the Femme Fatale

The fashion of the femme fatale is iconic, embodying a blend of sophistication, mystery, and undeniable allure. Her style is not just about appearance; it's a critical component of her identity, reflecting her confidence, control, and sensuality. The right wardrobe acts as armor and expression, projecting her strength and enhancing her presence. Here, we explore the key fashion essentials that define the femme fatale's iconic look, empowering any woman to channel this confidence in her personal style.

The Power of Color and Cut

A femme fatale knows the importance of color in fashion. Black, as the ultimate symbol of elegance and mystery, dominates her wardrobe. However, she might also incorporate deep reds or rich jewel tones, which signify passion and power. The choice of color is strategic, selected to evoke specific emotions and reactions.

The cut of her clothing is equally important. Tailored silhouettes that highlight her form without restricting movement are essential. She opts for garments that accentuate her strengths and communicate confidence, such as a well-fitted pencil skirt or a sharp blazer. Each piece is chosen to make a statement of self-assurance and poise.

If you have difficulties or doubts about how to match colors, here are some guidelines you can follow to best coordinate them.

Guidelines on How to Best Match Colors

1. **Monochromatic:** Using various shades of the same color can create a sophisticated and elegant look. For example, pairing different tones of blue can result in a harmonious effect.

2. **Complementary:** Complementary colors are opposite each other on the color wheel, such as blue and orange or red and green. Matching complementary colors can create a bold and dynamic look.

3. **Analogous:** Analogous colors are next to each other on the color wheel, like blue and green or red and orange. These combinations create a pleasing and relaxing effect.

4. **Neutral Accents:** Neutral colors such as black, white, gray, and beige can be used as a base to highlight more vibrant colors. For example, a black dress with red accessories.

5. **Contrast:** Using contrasting colors, such as a light dress with dark accessories, can add depth and visual interest to your outfit.

Jennifer Lopez is known for her glamorous style and sex appeal. Here's how she often matches colors in her outfits:

- **Formal Events:** Jennifer Lopez often chooses monochromatic outfits for formal events. For instance, a long white dress paired with silver jewelry, which highlights her tanned skin and creates an elegant and sophisticated look.

- **Red Carpet Looks:** For the red carpet, J.Lo loves bold and rich colors. An example is the famous green Versace dress that stunned everyone. In these occasions, she often pairs vibrant colors with metallic accessories, like gold or silver, for a luxurious and captivating look.

- **Casual Chic:** In her daily life, Jennifer Lopez opts for a casual yet refined style. She might wear skinny jeans with a white shirt and colorful accessories like a red bag or leopard print shoes. This balance between neutral and vibrant colors allows her to maintain an attractive yet relaxed style.

- **Performances:** During her performances, J.Lo often chooses sparkling costumes in metallic colors like gold or silver, often paired with black details for a dramatic and powerful look that captures attention.

By following these examples and guidelines, you can create outfits that not only highlight your best features but also communicate confidence and style,

Fabric Choices: Luxury and Comfort

Luxurious fabrics such as silk, velvet, and fine leather are staples in the femme fatale's wardrobe. These materials not only add a touch of glamour but also comfort, allowing her to move freely and with purpose. The tactile quality of her attire plays into the sensory aspects of her persona, leaving a lasting impression on those she encounters.

Classic Pieces with a Modern Twist

The femme fatale respects the power of classic fashion but also knows when to introduce a modern twist to keep her style fresh and relevant. A traditional trench coat might be reimagined in a high-gloss finish, or classic stiletto heels might feature unexpected textural details. She stays updated with trends but filters them through her unique aesthetic, ensuring her style remains timeless yet contemporary.

Kate Middleton, the Duchess of Cambridge, is a perfect example of a woman who seamlessly blends classic pieces with a modern twist. Here's how she does it:

- **Classic Dresses with Modern Details:** Kate often wears classic silhouettes like A-line dresses and tailored coats but chooses pieces with modern prints, textures, or embellishments. For instance, she might wear a timeless polka dot dress but with contemporary features like an asymmetric hem or bold color combinations.

- **Trench Coats with a Twist:** While Kate frequently wears traditional trench coats, she often opts for versions with unique details such as high-gloss finishes, contrasting collars, or unexpected colors like a deep burgundy or vibrant red. This keeps her outerwear looking fresh and interesting.

- **Updated Footwear:** Kate's shoe choices often reflect a balance between classic and modern. She might choose classic stiletto heels but with modern touches such as metallic finishes, textured materials, or unique patterns that add a contemporary edge to her look.

- **Mixing Traditional and Modern Accessories:** Kate is known for her impeccable accessorizing, blending classic and modern elements. She might pair a traditional pearl necklace with a trendy clutch bag or wear a vintage-inspired hat with a modern, structured dress.

- **Modern Prints and Fabrics:** Even when wearing classic cuts, Kate ensures her outfits stay current by choosing modern prints and fabrics. For example, she may wear a classic tailored coat in a bold tartan print or a structured dress in a luxurious, metallic fabric.

Accepting the fashion essentials of the femme fatale is about more than dressing up; it's about embracing an attitude. It's a celebration of self-expression and an assertion of one's presence in any room. For the modern woman looking to tap into her inner power, adopting these fashion principles can be a transformative experience, boosting confidence and asserting a sense of control in both her personal and professional life. By carefully selecting garments that resonate with the femme fatale spirit, any woman can harness the power of fashion to craft an image that is both powerful and captivating.

Makeup and Hairstyling Tips

Makeup and hairstyling are pivotal elements in the femme fatale's arsenal, tools that enhance her mystique and highlight her innate elegance. The right makeup and hairstyle not only complement her fashion choices but also reinforces her presence and persona. For anyone looking to embody this iconic archetype, mastering the art of makeup and hairstyling is essential. Let's explore how to achieve that perfect blend of allure and sophistication.

Strategic Makeup: Accentuate with Intention

The femme fatale's makeup is never left to chance; it's meticulously planned to accentuate her best features and set the tone for her intended impact. A flawless complexion is the foundation of her look, symbolizing both health and meticulous attention to detail. She opts for a matte or semi-matte base to maintain an elegant finish throughout the day or night.

Eyes are perhaps the most critical aspect of the femme fatale's makeup. Smoky eye makeup, using shades of charcoal, plum, or deep green, adds depth and intrigue, drawing others in. Eyeliner is applied with precision, with a winged tip to evoke a sense of boldness and drama. Mascara is used liberally to curl and define lashes, ensuring her gaze holds power and command.

Lips are another focal point. Depending on the occasion, she might choose a bold red lip to signify strength and passion or a more subdued nude or berry shade for understated elegance. The key is in the application—perfectly defined and filled for a polished look.

Hairstyling: Sleek, Polished, and Controlled

The femme fatale's hair is her crowning glory, styled to perfection to complement her overall appearance. Whether she opts for a sleek bob, soft waves, or a tight updo, her hairstyle is always impeccable and purposeful.

For those with longer hair, voluminous waves that cascade gracefully can add a touch of classic glamour, especially when paired with a striking outfit. The hair should look touchable but controlled, never messy or unstyled.

An example of a woman who embodies these characteristics is Blake Lively. Blake is known for her voluminous and flowing waves that add a touch of classic glamour to her look, especially when she wears stunning outfits on the red carpet. Her hair always appears polished and refined, with a natural and touchable look, but never messy or unstyled.

Shorter hairstyles, like a sharp bob or pixie cut, speak to a more modern femme fatale—chic, daring, and sophisticated. These styles are often paired with a striking hair color, such as jet black or rich brunette, to maintain an air of mystery.

An example is Charlize Theron. Charlize is known for her shorter hairstyles, such as the pixie cut and sharp bob, which give her a modern, daring, and sophisticated look. She often pairs these cuts with striking hair colors, like jet black or rich brunette, maintaining an air of mystery and allure.

Tips for Maintenance and Consistency

For the femme fatale, consistency in her appearance is key. Regular trims, deep conditioning treatments, and high-quality styling products are essential to maintaining the health and style of her hair. Similarly, investing in high-quality makeup that lasts through the day and into the night ensures she is always presenting her best self.

The makeup and hairstyling of the femme fatale are not just about beauty—they are about projecting strength, sophistication, and an unspoken promise of intrigue. By adopting these styling tips, anyone can channel the femme fatale's confidence and presence. Whether heading to a business meeting or a social event, the right makeup and hairstyle can make a powerful statement, empowering her to manage any scenario with poise and determination.

Accessorizing Like a Femme Fatale

Accessorizing is an art form for the femme fatale, with each choice serving as a subtle yet powerful expression of her identity and intentions. The right accessories not only complement her outfit but also enhance her presence, adding layers of intrigue and sophistication to her persona. From statement jewelry to the strategic use of scarves and handbags, each piece is selected with precision and purpose. Here's how to master the art of accessorizing in true femme fatale style.

Signature Jewelry: Bold and Meaningful

For the femme fatale, jewelry is never just ornamental; it's a statement of power and personality. A signature piece, such as a bold necklace or an elegant pair of chandelier earrings, can act as the focal point of her ensemble, drawing attention and making an unforgettable impression. These pieces are chosen for their striking designs and the confidence they inspire.

Rings and bracelets can be stacked for a look that's both luxurious and assertive. Each piece should have a story or significance, adding depth to her character and serving as a conversation starter. For instance, a vintage cocktail ring might hint at a mysterious past, while a modern geometric bracelet could signify her forward-thinking attitude.

Here are some examples of when and where to wear these striking accessories:

Bold Necklace

When to Wear:

- **Formal Events:** Galas, high-profile charity events, or black-tie affairs.

- **Evening Out:** High-end restaurants or exclusive cocktail parties.

Example:

- **Event:** Charity Gala

- **Ensemble:** A sleek, black evening gown.

- **Jewelry:** A bold, statement necklace with large, shimmering gemstones.

- **Impact:** The necklace draws attention to the neckline and face, exuding confidence and sophistication. It serves as a focal point, ensuring that all eyes are on her as she makes her entrance.

Elegant Chandelier Earrings

When to Wear:

- **Cocktail Parties:** Glamorous social gatherings or art gallery openings.

- **Romantic Dinners:** Upscale dining experiences.

Example:

- **Event:** Art Gallery Opening

- **Ensemble:** An elegant, off-the-shoulder dress.

- **Jewelry:** Long chandelier earrings that sparkle with every movement.

- **Impact:** The earrings frame her face beautifully and catch the light, adding an element of drama and elegance. They create a sense of mystery and allure as she engages in conversation and moves through the crowd.

Stacked Rings and Bracelets

When to Wear:

- **Professional Settings:** Important business meetings or networking events.

- **Casual Chic:** Stylish brunches or shopping in trendy districts.

Example:

- **Event:** Business Networking Event

- **Ensemble:** A tailored, chic pantsuit.

- **Jewelry:** Stacked rings on one hand and a combination of modern geometric bracelets on the other.

- **Impact:** The jewelry subtly conveys her assertive and forward-thinking attitude. The rings and bracelets add a touch of luxury and personal style, making her memorable and reinforcing her powerful presence.

Vintage Cocktail Ring

When to Wear:

- **Intimate Gatherings:** Dinner parties with close friends or family.

- **Sophisticated Soirees:** Exclusive private events.

Example:

- **Event:** Dinner Party

- **Ensemble:** A classic, fitted dress in a deep, rich color.

- **Jewelry:** A vintage cocktail ring with an intricate design.

- **Impact:** The ring hints at a mysterious past or a significant event, sparking curiosity and conversation. It might be an heirloom or a piece with historical significance, adding an air of intrigue and depth to her persona.

Modern Geometric Bracelet

When to Wear:

- **Innovative Conferences:** Tech or design industry events.

- **Fashion Forward Outings:** Trendy cafes or fashion shows.

Example:

- **Event:** Tech Conference

- **Ensemble:** A contemporary, stylish outfit with clean lines.

- **Jewelry:** A sleek, modern geometric bracelet.

- **Impact:** The bracelet signifies her progressive and forward-thinking attitude. It complements her modern ensemble and highlights her innovative spirit, making her stand out in a crowd of professionals.

Whether through a bold necklace at a gala or stacked rings and bracelets at a business event, each piece contributes to your enigmatic and captivating presence.

Handbags and Clutches: Practical and Stylish

The femme fatale selects her handbags with as much care as her attire, opting for styles that are both functional and fashionable. A sleek, structured handbag in fine leather adds a touch of class and professionalism, perfect for daytime engagements. For evening occasions, a clutch in a bold color or with intricate embellishments can elevate her look, serving both aesthetic and practical purposes.

The choice of color and material plays a significant role in conveying her mood and the setting. Darker shades like deep reds, blacks, and blues suggest sophistication and mystery, while metallic or textured finishes can add a touch of drama and luxury.

Scarves and Sunglasses: Mysterious and Protective

Scarves and sunglasses are indispensable tools in the femme fatale's accessory arsenal. A well-chosen scarf can transform an outfit, adding a burst of color or a touch of elegance depending on its fabric and pattern. It can also serve a practical purpose, offering warmth or acting as a stylish disguise when needed.

Sunglasses, particularly in classic styles like the aviator or cat-eye, do more than protect her eyes from the sun. They add an air of mystery, shielding her expressions and intentions, while enhancing her mystique and allure.

Footwear: The Foundation of Her Presence

No outfit is complete without the right footwear, and for the femme fatale, shoes are the foundation of her commanding presence. High heels are a staple, elongating her silhouette and adding a seductive sway to her walk. However, the style and comfort level are carefully balanced to ensure she remains poised and in control. Sleek boots, stiletto heels, and elegant flats are all chosen for their ability to combine function with style, making a statement while supporting her through every step.

Accessorizing like a femme fatale is about more than just choosing the right items; it's about curating pieces that enhance her narrative and empower her presence. Each accessory is selected to complement her strengths and showcase her unique style, ensuring that she remains unforgettable. By mastering this art, you can embody the femme fatale's confidence and charm, using accessories not just as embellishments, but as tools of empowerment and expressions of your personal story.

Chapter 5 - The Art of Seduction

Seduction is not merely a tactic for romantic conquest; it's a powerful tool for influence and persuasion in all areas of life. By understanding the dynamics of attraction and connection, you can captivate and engage others more effectively. This chapter explores the principles of seduction and how they can be applied to improve your social and professional interactions.

We'll discuss the importance of understanding what drives people and how to create meaningful connections through confidence, emotional engagement, and maintaining a sense of mystery. Additionally, we'll cover the nuances of verbal and non-verbal communication, including clarity, tone, and body language, and how to use these tools to make a lasting impression.

You will also learn the importance of keeping people wanting more by creating anticipation, providing continuous value, encouraging active participation, and leveraging the power of follow-up. These strategies will help you build lasting and meaningful connections that keep your relationships vibrant and dynamic.

Principles of Seduction

Seduction, often misunderstood merely as a tactic for romantic conquest, is fundamentally about influence and persuasion. It involves understanding the dynamics of attraction and connection and utilizing these insights to engage and captivate others. This chapter explores the principles of seduction, emphasizing how they can be applied not only in personal relationships but also in broader interactions to enhance your social and professional life.

Understanding Attraction Dynamics

At its core, seduction is about appealing to other people's emotions, desires, and psychological needs. The first principle of seduction is to develop a deep understanding of what drives people: their fears, desires, and aspirations. This understanding allows you to craft interactions that resonate on a personal level, making others feel seen, understood, and intrigued. It's about creating a connection that feels both exciting and safe.

In order to do that, you need to develop, as the foundation of everything, 3 solid pillars. These are the characteristics that distinguish the figure of the femme fatale from the rest of the people. In fact, we have already talked about this in Chapter 3 'Crafting Your Femme Fatale Persona'; for this reason, I will return to the topic very quickly, just to remind you where you need to focus.

These 3 pillars are:

1) The Power of Confidence

Confidence is key in seduction. It's about knowing your value and conveying it without arrogance. Confidence attracts, reassures, and sets the stage for genuine connections. It's about presenting yourself as someone who knows what you want, how you plan to get it and believes in your ability to achieve it. This assurance is compelling and draws people in, making them want to engage with you and what you offer.

2) Emotional Engagement

Engaging people emotionally is a vital principle of seduction. This involves sharing stories, revealing vulnerabilities appropriately, and expressing genuine interest in others' experiences and feelings. Emotional engagement makes interactions memorable and builds a foundation of trust and curiosity. It's about moving beyond superficial exchanges and promoting deeper connections that captivate and hold attention.

3) The Art of Mystery

Maintaining a sense of mystery is another essential principle of seduction. While transparency is important, keeping some things back allows others to wonder and speculate, which keeps them engaged. This doesn't mean being deceptive or elusive but rather sharing selectively to pique interest and leave others wanting to know more about you.

Verbal and Non-Verbal Communication

Effective communication is a fundamental aspect of influence and connection, whether in personal relationships, professional environments, or casual interactions. Mastering both verbal and non-verbal cues can significantly enhance your ability to engage and captivate others. This section explores the subtleties of these cues, explaining how to use them to create deeper connections and convey confidence, interest, and charisma.

Verbal Communication

Verbal communication play a crucial role in how we connect and influence others. The words you choose, the tone of your voice, and the pace at which you speak can all convey a range of emotions and intentions. Key aspects include:

1. **CLARITY AND BREVITY:** Being clear and concise with your language prevents misunderstandings and keeps the listener's attention focused. It shows respect for the listener's time and demonstrates your ability to think and communicate clearly.

Angela Merkel, former Chancellor of Germany, is known for her clear and concise communication. Her language is direct, her tone of voice measured, and her speaking pace deliberate, allowing her to convey her intentions clearly and maintain the audience's attention. These qualities demonstrate her respect for the listeners' time and her ability to think and communicate effectively.

Here are some examples of what to do and what not to do:

Planning a Date:

- **Don't:** "I was thinking maybe we could go out sometime this week if you're free. There's this new restaurant I've heard about, but I'm not sure if you'd like it. We could also do something else if you prefer."

- **Implication:** This ambiguous plan can be seen as indecisive and may lead to misunderstandings or a lack of enthusiasm for the date.

- **Do:** "Let's meet at 7 PM at the Italian restaurant on Main Street. It's my treat."

- **Implication:** This clear and concise plan shows confidence and respect for the other person's time, making the date setup straightforward and appealing.

Professional Email:

- **Don't:** "Hi team, I hope everyone is doing well. I wanted to let you know that due to some unforeseen circumstances, we have to move the meeting that was originally scheduled for tomorrow morning to a later time. After considering various options, we decided that 10 AM would be the best time. Please let me know if this works for you. Thanks a lot,"

- **Implication:** This long-winded message can cause frustration and potentially important details might be overlooked.

- **Do:** "Hi team, the meeting is rescheduled to 10 AM tomorrow due to a conflict. Please adjust your calendars accordingly. Thanks, Alex."

- **Implication:** This clear and concise message respects the team's time and ensures everyone understands the new meeting time without confusion.

Resolving a Conflict:

- **Don't:** "You know, the other day when you canceled our plans, it really made me upset because I was looking forward to it, and it seemed like you didn't care about our time together. I understand if you had something important come up, but it still hurt my feelings."

- **Implication:** This long-winded explanation can overwhelm the other person and make it harder to address the main issue effectively.

☐ **Do:** "I felt hurt when you canceled our plans last minute. Can we talk about it?"

☐ **Implication:** This clear communication addresses the issue without unnecessary details, allowing for a focused and productive conversation.

An exercise you can do to improve in this area is called daily summaries.

☐ **Task:** At the end of each day, write a summary of your day's main activities in no more than three sentences. Focus on the most important aspects and avoid unnecessary details.

☐ **Example:** "Today, I completed the client presentation, attended the team meeting to discuss project timelines, and responded to urgent emails. Preparing for tomorrow's client call is the next priority."

2. **THE TONE OF VOICE:** The tone can often convey more than

the actual words spoken. A warm, friendly, confident tone can put people at ease and draw them in, while a monotonous or harsh tone can push them away.

An example of a woman who embodies these characteristics is Malala Yousafzai. Malala is known for her warm, friendly, and confident tone of voice, which puts people at ease and draws them in. Her verbal communication skills have played a crucial role in her activism for girls' education and in her ability to inspire and mobilize people worldwide through her speeches and public appearances.

Real-Life Examples of Different Tones Leading to Different Outcomes

Scenario 1: Giving Feedback to a Colleague

- **Warm, Friendly Tone:** "I really appreciate your hard work on this project. There's just one small area where I think we can improve."

    - **Outcome:** The colleague feels valued and open to constructive criticism, leading to a positive change and a stronger working relationship.

- **Harsh, Monotonous Tone:** "You need to fix these mistakes."

    - **Outcome:** The colleague feels demotivated and unappreciated, possibly leading to resentment and a lack of improvement.

Scenario 2: Expressing Interest in Someone

- **Warm, Friendly Tone:** "I've really enjoyed spending time with you lately. You're such a wonderful person."

    - **Outcome:** The person feels appreciated and comfortable, leading to a deeper connection and increased interest in spending more time together.

- **Harsh, Monotonous Tone:** "I like you. Do you want to go out sometime?"

    o Outcome: The person may feel uncomfortable or uninterested due to the lack of enthusiasm and warmth, reducing the likelihood of a positive response.

What I recommend you do is an exercise called voice modulation.

Exercise: Voice Modulation Practice

1. **Choose a Passage:** Select a short passage from a book or an article that you find interesting.

2. **Record Yourself:** Read the passage aloud while recording your voice. Try to read it naturally the first time.

3. **Identify Emotions:** Listen to the recording and identify the emotions you want to convey (e.g., excitement, sincerity, confidence).

4. **Practice Different Tones:**

    o **Warm and Friendly:** Read the passage again, focusing on sounding warm and friendly. Smile as you speak; it can naturally warm your tone.

    o **Confident:** Read the passage with a focus on sounding confident. Stand up straight, project your voice, and emphasize key points.

    o **Avoid Monotone:** Practice varying your pitch and speed. Stress important words and pause at natural breaks to avoid sounding monotonous.

5. **Record and Compare:** Record yourself reading the passage in each tone. Listen to each recording and note the differences. Pay attention to which tone is most effective and where you can improve.

6. **Get Feedback:** Share your recordings with a friend or mentor

and ask for feedback on your tone. Practice incorporating their suggestions.

Now we can continue with the third key aspect:

3. **PACING AND PAUSING:** Controlling the speed of your speech and incorporating pauses can enhance the weight of your words. Pauses are powerful; they allow the listener to absorb what has been said and anticipate what is coming next, building a sense of drama and interest.

Meryl Streep is known for her extraordinary verbal communication skills, both in her film roles and in public speeches. The choice of words, the tone of her voice, and the controlled pace of her speech are key elements of her communication style. She masterfully uses pauses to emphasize her messages, allowing the audience to reflect and keeping their attention and interest high.

Here's a real-life example where having the right pace and using a pause could benefit you:

In a Relationship Argument:

What to Do:

- **Example:** During a heated discussion with your partner, you notice emotions are high. You say, "I understand you're upset... (pause for 3 seconds) Let's try to talk about this calmly."

- **Implication:** The pause allows both you and your partner to take a breath and reduce tension, promoting a more constructive conversation.

What Not to Do:

- **Example:** During a heated discussion with your partner, you quickly respond with, "I understand you're upset, let's try to talk about this calmly."

- **Implication:** Without the pause, your words may not have the same calming effect, and the conversation may continue to escalate without a chance to de-escalate.

Practical Exercise to Improve Pacing and Pausing
Exercise: The 5-Second Rule

1. **Preparation:**

    o   Choose a topic you're comfortable talking about for one minute (e.g., your favorite hobby, a recent trip, or a project at work).

2. **Practice:**

    o   Start a timer and begin talking about your chosen topic.

    o   Every time you reach the end of a sentence or complete a thought, pause for 5 seconds before continuing.

    o   Repeat this exercise daily, gradually reducing the pause time to 3 seconds, then 2 seconds.

3. **Reflection:**

    o   After each session, reflect on how the pauses made you feel and how you believe they might affect a listener. Did you feel more in control of your speech? Did you notice a difference in the clarity and impact of your words?

4. **Real-World Application:**

    o   Try to incorporate these pauses in your daily conversations. For example, during your next meeting or casual chat, consciously add pauses after key points.

By regularly practicing this exercise, you'll become more comfortable with pausing, making your speech more engaging and effective in various settings.

4. **EMPATHETIC LANGUAGE:** Using language that shows understanding and empathy can help strengthen connections. This involves actively listening to the other person and responding in a way that reflects their feelings and viewpoints.

Another famous woman who embodies the characteristics described in the text is Jacinda Ardern. The former Prime Minister of New Zealand is known for her empathetic and understanding use of language in her public communications. Ardern actively listens and responds in a way that reflects the feelings and viewpoints of others, creating strong connections and demonstrating influential and humane leadership.

Example Scenario for Practice: Imagine your partner comes home after a hard day at work and says, "I'm so exhausted and fed up with my job."

- **What to Do:** "I'm sorry you're feeling this way. It sounds like today was really tough for you. Is there anything I can do to help or would you like to talk more about it?"

- **What Not to Do:** "Everyone has bad days at work, it's not a big deal. Just relax and forget about it."

An empathetic response shows understanding, support, and a willingness to listen. This approach helps build trust, encourages open communication, and provides emotional relief. When you acknowledge and validate your partner's feelings, they feel heard and valued, which strengthens your relationship. It makes it easier for them to share their thoughts and emotions with you in the future.

In contrast, a non-empathetic response dismisses your partner's feelings. It discourages them from opening up and can create emotional distance between you. When their feelings are brushed aside, they might feel unsupported and misunderstood. This can lead to increased stress and potential conflicts, as your partner may feel that their emotions are not important to you.

Using empathetic language regularly can improve the quality of your relationships, creating a more supportive and understanding environment. Your partner will appreciate the effort you put into truly listening and responding to their needs, making your connection stronger and more resilient.

Practical Exercise to Develop Empathetic Language

Step 1: Active Listening Practice active listening by engaging in a conversation with a friend or family member. Focus entirely on what they are saying without interrupting. Nod, make eye contact, and use small verbal acknowledgments like "I see" or "Go on" to show you are listening.

Step 2: Reflective Responses After they finish speaking, reflect back what they have said in your own words. For example, "It sounds like you're really frustrated with how your project at work is going." This helps ensure you understood correctly and shows that you are engaged with their feelings.

Step 3: Empathetic Statements Respond with empathetic statements that acknowledge their feelings and offer support. Use phrases like, "That must be really difficult for you," or "I can understand why you feel that way."

Step 4: Avoiding Judgment and Advice Resist the urge to immediately offer solutions or judge their feelings. Sometimes, people just want to be heard and validated rather than fixed.

Step 5: Practice Regularly Regularly practice these steps in different conversations. The more you use empathetic language, the more natural it will become.

Non-Verbal Communication

Non-verbal cues often convey more information than verbal ones and are essential in the art of seduction and influence. These include:

1. **EYE CONTACT:** Maintaining appropriate eye contact signifies confidence and interest in the person you are communicating with. It can make conversations more personal and engaging.

Real-Life Examples: Do's and Don'ts

Example 1: Romantic Date

- **Do:** On a romantic date, maintain eye contact with your partner, especially when they are speaking or when you are sharing something personal.

    - **Implication:** This shows that you are genuinely interested in them and value what they are saying. It helps build a deeper emotional connection and trust.

- **Don't:** Frequently looking at your phone, around the room, or avoiding eye contact.

    - Implication: This can make your date feel undervalued or ignored. It might suggest that you are not fully present or interested, potentially ruining the romantic connection.

Example 2: Negotiation Meeting

- **Do:** In a business negotiation, maintain eye contact with the other party when presenting your terms and when listening to theirs.

    - **Implication:** It demonstrates that you are confident in your position and respectful of theirs. It can lead to a more productive and balanced negotiation outcome.

- **Don't:** Looking away or down when discussing critical points or when the other party is speaking.

o **Implication:** This can make you appear weak or unsure of your position, giving the other party leverage and potentially leading to an unfavorable outcome for you.

To understand how to best use eye contact, you might take inspiration from characters in certain movies and TV shows, such as:

1. **James Bond (Movies):** James Bond, portrayed by actors like Sean Connery and Daniel Craig, uses eye contact to convey confidence, charm, and control in various situations, from seductions to high-stakes negotiations.

2. **Harvey Specter (Suits):** Harvey Specter, played by Gabriel Macht, uses eye contact masterfully in the series "Suits" to dominate negotiations and intimidate opponents. His unwavering gaze projects confidence and assertiveness.

3. **Claire Underwood (House of Cards):** Claire Underwood, portrayed by Robin Wright, uses intense eye contact to assert power and influence in political and personal interactions, demonstrating control and unwavering determination.

Two of the most effective exercises for developing eye contact are Mirror Practice and Public Settings.

☐ **Mirror Practice:** Stand in front of a mirror and practice maintaining eye contact with your reflection. Speak about a topic you are passionate about for 2-3 minutes, ensuring you do not break eye contact.

☐ **Public Settings:** When in public, such as at a coffee shop or store, make a conscious effort to maintain eye contact with the cashier or barista during your interaction. Start with brief interactions and gradually extend the duration as you become more comfortable.

The second fundamental skill regarding non-verbal communication is:

2. **FACIAL EXPRESSIONS:** A genuine smile can make you appear more approachable, trustworthy, and attractive. Other facial expressions can equally convey a wide range of emotions, helping to communicate your feelings and reactions more effectively.

Real-Life Examples: Do's and Don'ts

In a Date:

Do: Imagine you're on a date. You're genuinely interested in the other person and want to make a positive impression. A genuine smile can make you appear more approachable and attractive. Smile warmly when they say something funny or interesting. Your eyes should crinkle slightly, and your mouth should curve naturally upwards. This will signal your interest and make the other person feel valued.

Implications:

- **Positive Impact:** Your date will feel more comfortable and open up more. They are likely to perceive you as friendly and trustworthy, leading to a more engaging and enjoyable conversation.

Don't: On the same date, if you frequently glance away, avoid smiling, or give only half-hearted smiles, you might appear disinterested or nervous. Your expressions might seem forced or insincere, which can make the other person uncomfortable.

Implications:

- **Negative Impact:** Your date might feel undervalued or think you're not interested. This can lead to awkwardness and a lack of connection, making the date less enjoyable and potentially unsuccessful.

In a Job Interview:

Do: In a job interview, maintaining positive facial expressions can convey confidence and attentiveness. Nod and smile naturally when the interviewer speaks. This shows that you are engaged and interested in what they are saying.

Implications:

- **Positive Impact:** The interviewer perceives you as confident, reliable, and interested in the role. This can significantly increase your chances of getting the job.

Don't: In the job interview scenario, if you avoid smiling or show a tense facial expression, it may signal lack of confidence or enthusiasm for the position.

Implications:

- **Negative Impact:** The interviewer might perceive you as insecure or untrustworthy, reducing your chances of being hired.

An example of a person who is very good at this art is:

Oprah Winfrey

Oprah is known for her warm and genuine smile. Her expressions of empathy and interest when interviewing guests make her appear approachable and trustworthy. She often uses her facial expressions to show understanding and connect with her audience.

Her genuine expressions have helped her build a strong rapport with her guests and audience, making her one of the most beloved figures in media.

To conclude, the exercise I recommend for improving facial expression is as simple as it is effective:

Practice different facial expressions in front of the mirror. Try to convey emotions such as happiness, interest, surprise, and empathy. Notice how your face changes with each emotion.

3. **GESTURES:** Purposeful gestures can emphasize what you are saying and convey enthusiasm and passion. However, it's important to ensure that your gestures are in sync with your words; otherwise, they can distract or confuse the listener.

Example 1: Business Presentation

Do: Imagine you're giving a business presentation. You use purposeful gestures like pointing to the key points on your slides, making open hand movements to include the audience, and nodding in agreement to emphasize important statements. This shows enthusiasm and helps the audience follow your narrative.

Don't: In contrast, if you fidget with your pen, constantly touch your face, or have closed-off body language (like crossed arms), you might distract your audience and come across as nervous or disinterested.

Implications: Using effective gestures makes your presentation engaging, builds your credibility, and keeps the audience's attention. Ineffective gestures can make you seem unprepared and disinterested, leading to a lack of engagement and possibly even a negative impression of your professional abilities.

Here is a list of people from whom you can take inspiration:

☐ **Michelle Obama:**

- Michelle Obama is known for her effective use of gestures. In her speeches, she uses open hand movements, leans slightly forward to show engagement, and makes direct eye contact, all of which convey confidence and passion.

☐Audrey Hepburn:

- In her films, Audrey Hepburn often used delicate, graceful gestures that matched her words and emotions perfectly. Her ability to use gestures effectively added to her charm and screen presence.

☐Daenerys Targaryen (Emilia Clarke) in "Game of Thrones":

- Emilia Clarke, portraying Daenerys Targaryen, uses strong, purposeful gestures that convey her authority and determination. Her gestures are always in sync with her words, reinforcing her character's leadership and resolve.

Practical Exercise to Develop This Skill

1. **Mirror Practice:**

   o Stand in front of a mirror and practice speaking on different topics. Pay attention to your gestures and body language. Try to use purposeful movements that emphasize your points.

2. **Record and Review:**

   o Record yourself during a practice presentation or conversation. Watch the recording and note the effectiveness of your gestures. Are they in sync with your words? Are they distracting or enhancing your message?

3. **Mindfulness:**

   o Throughout your day, be mindful of your gestures. Are they open and engaging, or are they closed and defensive? Make a conscious effort to adjust as needed.

Now let's move on to the fourth fundamental skill:

4. **POSTURE AND PROXIMITY:** The way you hold yourself speaks volumes about your confidence and attitude. An open, relaxed posture invites interaction, while closed-off body language can seem disengaging. Similarly, understanding and respecting personal space while managing proximity can impact how your presence is perceived.

What to Do and What Not to Do

1. Professional Setting:

WHAT TO DO:

- **Open Posture:** Sit or stand with your shoulders back, chest open, and arms relaxed at your sides. This conveys confidence and approachability.

- **Appropriate Proximity:** When talking to a colleague or a client, maintain a distance of about an arm's length. This respects personal space while keeping the interaction engaging.

WHAT NOT TO DO:

- **Closed Posture:** Crossing your arms, hunching your shoulders, or turning your body away can make you seem defensive or disinterested.

- **Invasive Proximity:** Standing too close can make others uncomfortable and seem intrusive, while standing too far can appear aloof or disinterested.

Implications:

- **Positive Outcome:** By maintaining an open posture and appropriate proximity, you're likely to be perceived as confident, respectful, and approachable, advancing better communication and relationships.

- **Negative Outcome:** Closed posture and inappropriate proximity can lead to misunderstandings, discomfort, and a perception of unprofessionalism or lack of interest.

2. Social Setting (Relationships):

WHAT TO DO:

- **Open Posture:** When talking to a friend or partner, face them directly, keep your arms uncrossed, and maintain eye contact. This shows that you are attentive and engaged.

- **Comfortable Proximity:** When sitting or standing near your partner, ensure that you are close enough to show interest and intimacy but not so close that it invades their personal space.

WHAT NOT TO DO:

- **Closed Posture:** Avoid crossing your arms or legs and turning your body away, as this can signal disinterest or discomfort.

- **Excessive Proximity:** Avoid standing too close as it can make the other person feel suffocated or uncomfortable, while too much distance might signal a lack of interest or connection.

Implications:

- **Positive Outcome:** Using open posture and maintaining a comfortable proximity can strengthen relationships, build trust, and enhance emotional connections.

- **Negative Outcome:** Closed posture and inappropriate proximity can create barriers, lead to miscommunication, and weaken the bond.

Real-Life Examples of Famous Figures

1. Princess Diana:

- **What She Did Well:** Known for her open and approachable posture, Princess Diana often leaned slightly forward when talking to people, showing genuine interest and empathy. She maintained a respectful proximity that made others feel comfortable and valued.

2. Wonder Woman (Gal Gadot in the movie):

- **What She Does Well:** In the film, Wonder Woman's posture is always confident and strong, with open shoulders and a firm stance. This not only conveys her strength but also her openness and readiness to engage, making her a formidable and inspiring character.

Practical Exercise to Develop This Skill

Exercise: Mirror Practice

1. **Find a Mirror:** Stand in front of a full-length mirror.

2. **Practice Open Posture:** Stand with your feet shoulder-width apart, shoulders back, chest open, and arms relaxed. Practice smiling and making eye contact with your reflection.

3. **Simulate Interactions:** Imagine different scenarios (work meeting, casual chat with a friend, date with a partner) and practice how you would stand or sit. Adjust your posture and proximity as needed.

4. **Observe and Adjust:** Notice any habits like crossing arms or leaning away, and consciously correct them.

5. **Daily Practice:** Spend 5-10 minutes each day practicing this. Gradually incorporate these postures into real-life interactions.

Another interesting technique, whether your goal is to build rapport with the person in question, be it a work relationship or a romantic relationship, is mirroring—an interesting technique that you can integrate.

is a technique where you subtly copy the body language of the person you are interacting with.

This may enhance empathy and understanding, signaling a sense of alignment and rapport. Practice this technique in conversations by subtly aligning your posture, gestures, or facial expressions with those of your conversational partner. This doesn't mean mimicking every move but rather reflecting a general posture or mood. It's a strategy that increase connectivity and trust, reflecting the femme fatale's ability to engage deeply and meaningfully with others.

Integrating verbal and non-verbal communication effectively requires practice and awareness. The congruence between what you say and how you say it improves your authenticity and persuasiveness.

Gaining proficiency in both verbal and non-verbal communication is crucial for anyone seeking to improve their personal and professional relationships. By being mindful of how you use these cues and continually refining your communication skills, you can increase your influence, deepen your connections, and handle social interactions more successfully.

Keep Them Wanting More

The art of leaving people wanting more is a subtle yet powerful aspect of interpersonal dynamics and influence. This skill is especially valuable in contexts ranging from business networking to personal relationships. It involves balancing engagement and intrigue, ensuring that each interaction leaves a lasting impression and a desire to reconnect. Now i share with you the strategies to develop lasting interest and maintain engagement over time, effectively keeping people invested and eager for more.

Create a Sense of Anticipation

One of the keys to keeping people wanting more is creating a sense of anticipation. In storytelling, this might mean ending a conversation with a cliffhanger or an intriguing hint about future developments. In professional contexts, it might involve teasing upcoming projects or innovations without revealing too much detail. The goal is to make others feel that there is more to be discovered, which can keep them engaged and looking forward to future interactions.

Methods and Strategies

1. Use Intriguing Statements:

- Instead of finishing your thoughts completely, leave room for curiosity. For example, "I've got a fascinating story from last weekend. I'll tell you more about it later."

2. Tease Future Plans:

- Mention interesting plans or activities without revealing too much. For example, "I'm planning something fun for us next weekend. You'll love it."

3. Ask Engaging Questions:

- Stimulate curiosity by asking thought-provoking questions. For example, "Have you ever tried something totally unexpected that changed your perspective?"

4. Offer Limited Information:

- Share just enough to spark interest without giving everything away. For example, "There's something I've been wanting to share with you. It's quite special, but I think I'll save it for later."

5. Use Time-Based Hooks:

- Set expectations for future interactions. For example, "I have a surprise for you, but you'll have to wait until our next date."

6. Highlight Unique Insights:

- Make others feel special by hinting at exclusive information.

For example, "I've discovered something amazing recently, and I think you're the only one who'll appreciate it."

Conversational Phrases to Use

- "I have an interesting story about that, but let's save it for our next date."

- "You'll never guess what happened next... I'll tell you all about it later."

- "I'm planning something exciting for us, but you'll have to wait to find out."

- "There's more to this, but I don't want to give it all away now."

- "I've got a surprise for you that you're going to love, but it's for next time."

Examples of Everyday Situations

1. **First Date:**

- **Scenario:** You're on a first date and want to leave a lasting impression.

- **Example:** "I've been to some amazing places recently. I'd love to tell you about one of them, but let's save that story for our next date."

2. **Catching Up with a Friend:**

- Scenario: You're having coffee with a friend and want to keep the conversation lively.

- Example: "I started a new hobby that's been incredibly exciting. I have some great stories to share, but I'll save them for our next catch-up."

3. **Messaging:**

- **Scenario:** You're texting someone you're interested in.

- **Example:** "Guess what? I had the most interesting experience today. Can't wait to tell you about it when we see each other."

4. **Planning a Date:**

- Scenario: You're planning a date and want to build excitement.

- Example: "I've got a fun surprise planned for our date this weekend. You're going to love it, but I won't spoil the surprise now."

Example of Creating Anticipation in Daily Life

Scenario: Laura is getting to know Mark, someone she met at a social event. They are texting and planning their first date.

Laura: "I've discovered this amazing little spot that I think you'd love. It's a bit of a secret, but I'll take you there next weekend."

Mark: "Sounds intriguing! What kind of place is it?"

Laura: "I don't want to ruin the surprise. Trust me, it's worth the wait. You'll see next Saturday."

Implication: By teasing the secret spot without giving away details, Laura builds anticipation and keeps Mark excited and curious about their upcoming date. This approach creates a sense of intrigue and makes their interactions more engaging and memorable.

Using these strategies and methods can effectively create a sense of anticipation, ensuring that people remain engaged and look forward to their next interaction with you

Provide Value Continuously

To keep people coming back, consistently provide value in your interactions. This could be practical advice, emotional support, unique insights, or even entertainment. The key is to make your presence beneficial to others in some way. When people know that time spent with you is time well spent, they will naturally want to maintain the connection. This principle applies equally to personal relationships and professional networks; always aim to contribute positively and meaningfully.

But be careful:

When it comes to providing value in relationships and keeping people wanting more, it's crucial to strike a balance. This doesn't mean that you should bend over backward to please others at the expense of your own needs and well-being. Instead, you should aim to contribute positively and meaningfully while also being true to yourself. Here's how to master this balance effectively.

Understanding the Importance of Balance

Firstly, it's essential to recognize that constantly trying to please others can lead to burnout and a loss of self-identity. You might find yourself saying "yes" to everything, always putting others' needs before your own, and feeling drained as a result. This is neither sustainable nor healthy. Genuine connections thrive on mutual respect and understanding, not on one person continuously sacrificing their own needs to accommodate the other.

Practical Strategies for Maintaining Balance

1. Be Genuine:

- Authenticity is attractive and builds deeper connections. When you share your true interests and passions, you not only enrich the conversation but also stay true to yourself. For instance, if you love hiking, invite someone to join you on a trail you enjoy. This way, you're sharing a part of your life that brings you joy.

2. **Set Boundaries:**

- It's perfectly okay to set limits on your availability and what you're willing to do. Respecting your own time and energy is crucial. If you're feeling overwhelmed, it's better to be honest about it. For example, you might say, "I'd love to help you with that, but I need to finish my own tasks first. Can we look at it together tomorrow?"

3. **Offer Help Selectively:**

- While being helpful is a great trait, doing so selectively ensures that you're not overextending yourself. Offer assistance when you genuinely want to and when you have the capacity to do so. For example, "I know you're working on that project. If you need someone to brainstorm with, I'm available on Thursday."

4. **Value Mutual Exchange:**

- Relationships should be reciprocal. Just as you offer support, be open to receiving it. This mutual exchange strengthens the bond and ensures that both parties feel valued. For example, if a friend offers advice or help, accept it graciously and reciprocate when you can.

5. **Communicate Openly:**

- Honest communication is the foundation of healthy relationships. Sharing your thoughts and feelings openly prevents misunderstandings and ensures that both parties are on the same page. For instance, "I really enjoy spending time with you, but I also need some alone time to recharge. Let's plan something for next weekend."

Balancing Value in Real-Life Scenarios

1. **In Romantic Relationships:**

- You might love spending time with your partner, but it's

essential to maintain your individuality. For example, "I love our time together, but I've planned a night with my friends. Let's do something special on Saturday."

2. When Building New Connections:

- It's tempting to be overly accommodating when trying to impress someone new, but showing that you have your own priorities is also important. For example, "I had a great time at dinner. I'm really looking forward to our next date, but I have a busy week ahead. How about we plan for Friday?"

3. With Friends:

- Supporting a friend in need is crucial, but so is taking care of yourself. For example, "I know you're having a tough time, and I'm here for you. I have some commitments this week, but let's catch up properly on the weekend."

4. In Professional Settings:

- Being a helpful colleague is valuable, but not at the cost of your own work. For example, "I'd love to help with your report. I have a few deadlines today, but I can assist you tomorrow afternoon."

Encourage Active Participation

Engagement is a two-way street. Encouraging others to participate actively in your interactions makes them more invested in the relationship. Ask questions, solicit opinions, and invite others to share their experiences and thoughts. This involvement makes the interaction more collaborative and engaging, deepening the connection and making your conversations more memorable. People are more likely to look forward to interactions where they feel genuinely heard and valued.

Here are some practical methods and conversational techniques to achieve this:

1. Ask Open-Ended Questions

Open-ended questions require more than a yes or no answer, encouraging the other person to share more about themselves.

- Examples:

    o "What do you enjoy most about your work?"

    o "Can you tell me more about your recent trip?"

    o "What are your thoughts on the latest project we're working on?"

2. Show Genuine Interest and Curiosity

Demonstrate that you are genuinely interested in what the other person is saying. Use follow-up questions and express curiosity.

- Examples:

    o "That's fascinating! How did you get into that hobby?"

    o "Wow, that sounds challenging. How did you manage to overcome that?"

    o "Tell me more about how you developed that skill."

3. Acknowledge and Validate Their Responses

People feel valued when their thoughts and feelings are acknowledged and validated.

- Examples:

    o "I can see why you feel that way."

    o "That makes a lot of sense."

o   "I appreciate you sharing that with me."

4. Invite Their Opinions and Ideas

Encourage them to share their viewpoints and contribute to the conversation.

- **Examples:**

    o   "What do you think about this approach?"

    o   "I'd love to hear your perspective on this issue."

    o   "Do you have any suggestions on how we can improve this?"

The final point to ensure that you keep them wanting more is:

Leverage the Power of Follow-Up

Finally, the art of follow-up is crucial in maintaining interest. Whether it's a simple "thank you" message, a check-in to continue a conversation, or an update on a topic discussed previously, following up shows that you value the relationship and are committed to keeping it alive. This not only reinforces the connection but also keeps you on their mind, effectively maintaining a sense of ongoing engagement.

Leveraging the Power of Follow-Up

1. Timely Follow-Up

- **Practical Method:** Send a follow-up message within a day or two after your interaction. Mention something specific from your conversation to show you were attentive.

- **Examples:** "It was great discussing [topic] with you," "I enjoyed our conversation about [specific detail]," "Thank you for sharing your insights on [topic]."

2. Check-In Messages

- **Practical Method:** Periodically check in with the person to continue the conversation or simply to show you care.

- **Examples:** "How have you been since we last talked?" "I was thinking about our discussion on [topic] and wanted to see how things are going," "Hope all is well with you."

3. Provide Value

- **Practical Method:** Share articles, resources, or information that you think the other person might find valuable based on your previous conversations.

- **Examples** "I came across this article and thought of you," "Here's a resource you might find helpful," "Remember our talk about [topic]? Check this out."

4. Express Gratitude

- **Practical Method:** Regularly thank the person for their time, insights, or any help they provided. Gratitude strengthens bonds and keeps you memorable.

- **Examples** "Thank you for your time," "I appreciate your insights," "Your advice was invaluable."

5. Plan Future Interactions

- **Practical Method:** Suggest meeting up again or continuing the conversation at a later date. This sets the stage for ongoing engagement.

- **Examples** "Let's catch up again soon," "I'd love to continue our discussion," "How about we meet up next week to talk more about this?"

Keeping them wanting more is about achieving the balance between sharing and reserving, giving and holding back. By creating anticipation, developing an aura of mystery, providing continuous value, encouraging participation, and following up effectively, you can keep others engaged and interested over time. These strategies are essential for building lasting and meaningful connections that both fulfill and inspire continued interaction. Whether in personal or professional settings, these techniques can strengthen your influence and ensure your relationships remain vibrant and dynamic.

Chapter 6 – Mastering Social Dynamics

Understanding and steering social situations with grace and effectiveness is a crucial skill for achieving personal and professional success. This chapter will explore how you can improve your social fluency and achieve your goals by drawing on the psychological sophistication and strategic acumen associated with the femme fatale archetype. We will discuss key techniques for managing social dynamics, building meaningful relationships, and handling competition and opposition with finesse.

From recognizing the social landscape and adapting your communication style to leveraging emotional intelligence and strategic influence, you'll learn practical methods to handle various social scenarios. We will also examine how to use persuasion ethically and effectively, including the power of storytelling and metaphors. Additionally, you'll gain insights into handling conflicts and transforming competition into opportunities for growth.

By integrating these principles, you can increase your ability to influence outcomes, build robust networks, and thrive in diverse social environments. This chapter lays the foundation for advanced interpersonal strategies that will empower you to excel in any social setting.

Steering Social Situations

Steering social situations with grace and effectiveness is an essential skill, particularly when your goals involve influencing outcomes or building strategic relationships. Drawing upon the psychological sophistication and strategic acumen often associated with the femme fatale archetype, we can uncover powerful techniques for managing and mastering various social dynamics. This approach not only increases our social fluency but also enhances our ability to achieve personal and professional objectives through adept social navigation.

The first step in effectively steering social situations is a deep understanding of the social landscape. This involves more than just reading the room; it means developing a nuanced awareness of the cultural, emotional, and interpersonal currents that influence social interactions. Recognizing these dynamics allows you to anticipate reactions and tailor your approaches to fit the context and the specific needs and personalities of those involved.

Effective social navigation requires building relationships that are both meaningful and strategic. This involves identifying key persons whose interests align with your own and promoting mutually beneficial connections. Approach relationship building with authenticity—people are adept at detecting insincerity, and genuine connections yield longer-lasting and more fruitful interactions. However, keep your strategic objectives in mind; consider what each relationship can bring to both parties and how these alliances can support your broader goals. Adapting your communication style to fit different audiences is crucial. This doesn't mean losing your voice or changing your personality, but rather adjusting your delivery to better connect with others.

Making subtle changes to your tone, language, or even the speed of your delivery can significantly influence the reception of your message. Effective communicators are those who can convey their ideas in a way that resonates with a diverse array of people, making them feel understood and valued.

High emotional intelligence is pivotal in steering through social situations. It allows you to manage not only your emotions but also to empathize with others, interpreting and reacting to their emotional states in a way that encourage positive interactions. This skill is especially crucial in handling conflicts or delicate situations where comprehension and tact are essential. By effectively managing emotions, you can maintain composure and assertiveness without alienating others, turning potential confrontations into constructive dialogues.

Influence is not about manipulation but about understanding what drives people and how to align those drives with your goals. Techniques such as reciprocity, commitment, and social proof can be tactfully employed to guide outcomes subtly and respectfully. Being aware of these dynamics and using them ethically and effectively can transform your social strategy, enabling you to move fluidly and successfully through complex networks.

It requires a blend of empathy, strategic thinking, and genuine interpersonal engagement. By understanding and applying these principles, you can enhance your ability to influence outcomes and build robust networks that are beneficial for all parties involved. The skills of the femme fatale—understanding human nature, strategic planning, emotional intelligence, and influential communication—offer valuable lessons for anyone looking to excel in social environments. As we continue to explore techniques in influence and persuasion and strategies for handling competition and opposition, these foundational skills will serve as the bedrock for advanced interpersonal strategies.

Influence and Persuasion Techniques applied in social situations

In addition to all the techniques already explained in previous chapters, regarding social contexts, there are some fundamental principles you should consider because they could be very helpful.

These principles, researched extensively by social psychologists, provide a framework for developing persuasive strategies that are both ethical and effective:

- **Authority:** Establishing yourself as a credible, knowledgeable authority in a particular area can significantly influence how people respond to your messages. Authority is not about wielding power but about demonstrating expertise and building trust.

- **Consistency:** People generally strive to align their current actions and behaviors with what they have previously expressed or demonstrated. Persuasion can often involve encouraging others to act in ways that align with their existing commitments and values.

- **Liking:** People are more likely to be influenced by others whom they like. Building rapport and showing genuine interest in others can enhance your influence.

- **Consensus:** Showing that others are taking a course of action encourages others to follow suit, leveraging the power of social proof.

- **Reciprocity:** People tend to return a favor. By being the first to give—whether it be a piece of knowledge, a positive experience, or a tangible benefit—you create a sense of indebtedness that can gently encourage others to reciprocate.

Furthermore, effective persuasion requires clear, compelling communication. Your ability to articulate ideas clearly and excitingly can make a significant difference in how your messages are received and acted upon. To communicate with impact:

- **Use stories and metaphors:** Stories captivate the emotions and stimulate the imagination of the listener, rendering your message more impactful and memorable.

For example, look at how the way the message is received changes:

Without Storytelling and Metaphors

Simple message: "Consistently working hard leads to success. Even when it seems difficult, continuing to work hard is important."

With Storytelling and Metaphors: "Once upon a time, there was a young woman named Anna who dreamed of becoming a famous pianist. Every day, Anna woke up before dawn to practice, even when her hands were tired and sore. Her friends teased her, saying she was wasting her time. But Anna knew that her dedication was like water slowly carving through rock: one day, it would make a difference. Years went by, and Anna never stopped practicing. Eventually, her talent was discovered by a famous conductor, and Anna played in front of thousands of people. Her constant effort had turned her into a shining star in the world of music."

Difference and Impact

The simple statement, "Consistently working hard leads to success. Even when it seems difficult, continuing to work hard is important," is clear but flat. It conveys the message directly but lacks emotional depth and engagement. While it is easy to understand, it does not leave a lasting impression.

In contrast, Anna's story is engaging and vivid. The narrative creates a vivid and emotionally engaging image, drawing the reader in. The use of the metaphor "water slowly carving through rock" adds a visual and conceptual dimension that makes the message more memorable. This metaphor not only illustrates Anna's perseverance but also enhances the reader's understanding and retention of the message.

Furthermore, the story is emotionally resonant. It allows the reader to empathize with Anna, making the message about hard work and perseverance more powerful and inspiring. By connecting emotionally with the character, the reader is more likely to internalize and be moved by the message.

Lastly, storytelling makes the message memorable. People remember stories and images more easily than simple statements. Anna's story stays in the reader's mind, reinforcing the original message more effectively. The vivid imagery and emotional connection ensure that the lesson about perseverance and hard work is not only understood but also remembered.

By applying these techniques thoughtfully and ethically, you can improve your interpersonal effectiveness, leading to more positive and productive outcomes. As we move on to explore how to handle competition and opposition, these persuasion skills will be crucial for handling challenges and turning potential conflicts into opportunities for collaboration and consensus.

Handling Competition and Opposition

Coursing through competition and opposition is a crucial skill in both personal and professional realms. It involves understanding the dynamics at play, maintaining your composure, and strategically managing conflicts to transform potential threats into opportunities for growth and collaboration. Drawing on the cunning and strategic prowess often attributed to the femme fatale archetype, this chapter explores how to handle competitive scenarios with finesse and effectiveness.

The first step in effectively handling competition is to understand its nature. Competition can arise from differing goals, resource limitations, or simply from the inherent conflict of interests that occurs in diverse environments. Recognizing the underlying reasons for opposition can provide insights into how to approach these challenges constructively:

Assess the landscape: Understanding the motivations and strengths of your competitors can help you predict their moves and prepare your responses.

For example:

Queen Elizabeth I's reign is a prime example of effective landscape assessment leading to victory. When she ascended the throne in 1558, England faced religious turmoil and threats from powerful nations like Spain.

Elizabeth recognized King Philip II of Spain as her most formidable opponent, motivated by a desire to reassert Catholic dominance. Spain's strengths included a powerful navy and vast wealth. Predicting Philip's moves, Elizabeth reinforced England's navy, building faster, more maneuverable ships, and worked to unify her people through religious reforms.

Her strategic acumen culminated in the defeat of the Spanish Armada in 1588. The massive Spanish fleet intended to invade England, but Elizabeth's preparations allowed the smaller, more agile English ships to outmaneuver the Spanish, leading to a decisive victory. This triumph bolstered Elizabeth's authority and cemented her status as a formidable leader, ushering in the prosperous Elizabethan Era.

Queen Elizabeth I's ability to assess the competitive landscape and prepare strategic responses ensured her reign's success and stability. Her victory over the Spanish Armada highlights the power of strategic foresight in achieving decisive outcomes.

Leverage: Understanding the specific needs and objectives that drive your competitors can offer you leverage in negotiations and interactions. By comprehending what they value or fear, you can tailor your strategies to position yourself more favorably.

Best Questions to Understand Needs and Objectives

1. **Personal Goals and Aspirations**

   o "What are your most important personal goals right now?"

   o "What do you hope to achieve in the next few years in your personal life?"

2. **Challenges and Obstacles**

   o "What are the biggest challenges you're currently facing in your life?"

   o "What are the things that worry you the most day-to-day?"

3. **Priorities and Values**

   o "What do you value most in life?"

o   "What are your top priorities at this stage of your life?"

4. **Success and Fulfillment**

o   "How do you define success and fulfillment in your personal life?"

o   "What experiences or achievements make you feel truly satisfied?"

5. **Motivations**

o   "What motivates you to pursue your personal goals?"

o   "What keeps you going when you face difficulties?"

6. **Fears and Concerns**

o   "What are your biggest fears about the future?"

o   "What aspects of life concern you the most?"

7. **Needs and Resources**

o   "What do you feel you need more of in your life to be happy?"

o   "Are there specific resources or support that would help you achieve your personal goals?"

8. **Past Experiences**

o   "Can you share a personal experience where you overcame a significant challenge?"

o   "What have been your most rewarding experiences in life so far?"

9. **Relationships and Social Connections**

o   "Who are the most important people in your life, and why?"

o   "How do your relationships impact your personal goals and happiness?"

10. **Expectations and Desires**

    o   "What are your expectations for the future?"

    o   "What outcomes are you hoping to achieve in your personal life?"

By asking these questions, you can gain a deeper understanding of what drives the person you're interacting with in their everyday life. This knowledge allows you to tailor your interactions and support to align with their needs and objectives, providing leverage in personal relationships and promoting more effective and mutually fulfilling connections.

Build alliances: Sometimes, the best way to handle competition is through strategic partnerships. Identifying potential allies can dilute the impact of opposition and increase your influence and resources. Collaborations can convert competitors into partners, building a network that benefits all involved parties.

Strategic Conflict Management

Dealing with opposition (whether in relationships or at work) requires tact and strategic conflict management. The aim is to mitigate conflict in a way that preserves relationships and promotes mutual benefits:

- **Stay composed:** Maintain your composure and keep your emotions in check. This not only helps in thinking clearly but also in projecting confidence and control, which can be crucial in negotiations. I won't dwell on this point too much because I've already given you practical advice about it in previous chapters.

- **Choose your battles:** Not every conflict is worth engaging.

Assess the significance of the disagreement and decide if it merits confrontation or if it can be resolved through compromise or by agreeing to disagree.

Asking yourself these questions before engaging in a conflict can be helpful:

☐ **How Important Is This Issue?**

- "Will this matter in the long run?"

☐ **What Are the Potential Consequences?**

- "What might happen if I avoid this conflict?"

☐ **How Will This Affect My Relationship?**

- "Is this worth potentially damaging my relationship with the other person?"

Do I Have the Energy and Resources?

- "Do I have the emotional and mental energy to engage in this conflict effectively?"

- Use active listening: Often, opposition is rooted in misunderstandings. By attentively listening, you can grasp the other party's perspective and effectively address the underlying issues. This can pave the way for more effective solutions and reduce antagonism.

Finally, viewing competition as an opportunity rather than a threat can transform how you handle challenges. Competition can be a powerful motivator for growth, innovation, and improvement:

- **Learn from your competitors:** Use competition as a chance to learn and adapt. Observing how others handle similar challenges can provide valuable insights that you can apply in your context.

- **Strengthen your position:** Each competitive scenario provides a chance to refine your strategies and strengthen your position. Use these experiences to build resilience and enhance your capabilities.

Handling competition and opposition effectively requires a blend of strategic thinking, emotional intelligence, and persuasive communication. By applying these skills, you can handle conflicts with grace, turn challenges into opportunities for collaboration, and encourage an environment where competition drives innovation and growth. This proactive approach not only positions you more favorably in any professional landscape but also contributes to a more dynamic and productive personal life. As you continue to refine these skills, you'll find that your ability to manage and leverage competition becomes a significant advantage in achieving your goals.

Chapter 7 - Intellectual and Emotional Strength

In this chapter, we'll discover the vital importance of intellectual curiosity and emotional resilience. These qualities drive personal growth, help you adapt to change, and enhance your ability to face life's challenges with confidence. By expanding your knowledge and understanding your emotions, you can make smarter decisions and build stronger relationships. This chapter will guide you through practical steps to nurture these strengths, including diversifying your reading habits, engaging in discussions, traveling, and developing self-sufficiency. You'll also explore the profound impact of these traits on your personal and professional life, highlighting how they contribute to a more fulfilling and empowered existence.

Building Intellectual Curiosity and Knowledge

Intellectual curiosity and the pursuit of knowledge are foundational traits for personal growth and success. These characteristics empower people to explore new ideas, challenge conventional wisdom, and continually adapt to an ever-changing world. In this chapter, we will probe into the importance of nurturing intellectual curiosity and how expanding one's knowledge base can lead to profound personal and professional achievements.

At the core of intellectual curiosity is the desire to explore and understand the world beyond the familiar and the known. It involves a proactive approach to learning, where questions are welcomed and the search for answers becomes a compelling journey. This mindset is akin to turning life into a vibrant classroom where every experience and interaction has something to teach us.

One effective way to encourage this mindset is to embrace the concept of lifelong learning. This means seeing education not as a finite period that ends with graduation but as a continuous, ever-evolving process. Engaging with diverse subjects, learning new skills, and exposing oneself to different perspectives are all part of building a broad and resilient intellectual foundation.

Critical thinking is an invaluable skill in the toolkit of the intellectually curious. It involves not merely absorbing information but analyzing, questioning, and evaluating it to form reasoned judgments. This skill enables people to sift through the vast amounts of information available today, discerning fact from opinion and truth from misinformation.

Developing critical thinking starts with adopting skepticism about the status quo and a readiness to challenge one's own beliefs and assumptions. It's about asking not just "what" or "how," but "why." This questioning attitude helps in refining one's thoughts and promotes a deeper understanding of complex issues.

When you invest in your intellect, you are not just learning new things; you are also building your capacity to make smarter decisions, solve problems more effectively, and think more creatively. This empowerment through knowledge enhances your ability to influence your environment positively.

The more you know, the more you trust your ability to face whatever challenges come your way. This knowledge-based confidence is not just about having facts at your fingertips but about feeling equipped to handle uncertainty and complexity.

Practical Steps to Enhance Intellectual Curiosity

1. **DIVERSIFY YOUR READING HABITS -** Venture beyond your usual preferences. If you typically read fiction, try non-fiction books on subjects like science, history, or economics. If you lean towards technical materials, explore poetry or philosophy.

Below, I share what I consider to be the most interesting books I've read on various topics:

For Fiction Readers Exploring Non-Fiction:

1. **Science:**

   o *Sapiens: A Brief History of Humankind* by Yuval Noah Harari

   o *The Gene: An Intimate History* by Siddhartha Mukherjee

2. **History:**

   o *Guns, Germs, and Steel: The Fates of Human Societies* by Jared Diamond

   o *The Silk Roads: A New History of the World* by Peter Frankopan

3. **Economics:**

   o *Freakonomics: A Rogue Economist Explores the Hidden Side of Everything* by Steven D. Levitt and Stephen J. Dubner

   o *Capital in the Twenty-First Century* by Thomas Piketty

For Non-Fiction Readers Exploring Fiction:

1. **Poetry:**

   o *The Sun and Her Flowers* by Rupi Kaur

   o *Leaves of Grass* by Walt Whitman

2. **Philosophy:**

   o *The Alchemist* by Paulo Coelho (philosophical fiction)

   o *Sophie's World* by Jostein Gaarder (novel about the history of philosophy)

3. **Literary Fiction:**

- o   *To Kill a Mockingbird* by Harper Lee

- o   *One Hundred Years of Solitude* by Gabriel García Márquez

For Technical Readers Exploring Creative Works:

1. **Philosophy:**

   - o   *Zen and the Art of Motorcycle Maintenance: An Inquiry into Values* by Robert M. Pirsig

   - o   *The Republic* by Plato

2. **Poetry:**

   - o   *The Waste Land* by T.S. Eliot

   - o   *The Essential Rumi* by Rumi

3. **Literature:**

   - o   *1984* by George Orwell

   - o   *The Great Gatsby* by F. Scott Fitzgerald

For Fiction Lovers Trying Non-Fiction:

1. **Science:**

   - o   *A Brief History of Time* by Stephen Hawking

   - o   *The Immortal Life of Henrietta Lacks* by Rebecca Skloot

2. **History:**

   - o   *The Wright Brothers* by David McCullough

   - o   *The Diary of a Young Girl* by Anne Frank

3. Self-Help:

   o *The Power of Habit: Why We Do What We Do in Life and Business* by Charles Duhigg

   o *Thinking, Fast and Slow* by Daniel Kahneman

Diversifying your reading habits not only broadens your knowledge but also stimulates intellectual curiosity by exposing you to different perspectives and fields of study. Whether you are a fiction aficionado exploring the depths of science and history or a technical reader delving into the beauty of poetry and philosophy, these books offer a rich array of intellectual experiences.

2. **ENGAGE IN DISCUSSIONS AND DEBATES** - Engaging in dialogue with others exposes you to diverse perspectives and compels you to articulate and defend your own ideas, thereby enhancing your critical thinking skills and broadening your understanding.

Besides this, you might want to take a look at these platforms:

Online Forums and Communities:

1. **Reddit:** Subreddits like r/ChangeMyView and r/TrueReddit offer platforms for thoughtful debates and discussions on a wide range of topics.

2. **Quora:** A question-and-answer platform where people discuss various subjects, providing insights and different perspectives.

Debate Websites and Platforms:

1. **Kialo:** A debate platform designed to facilitate thoughtful discussion and debate on complex topics.

2. **Debate.org:** A website where users can engage in debates on a variety of topics and vote on the outcomes.

Educational Platforms:

1. **Coursera and edX:** Many courses include discussion forums where students can engage in debates on course-related topics.

2. **The Great Courses Plus:** Offers courses with forums for discussion, where you can engage with fellow learners.

Watching Debates:

YouTube Channels:

1. **Intelligence Squared:** A platform that hosts live debates and discussions on contemporary issues, available to watch on their YouTube channel.

2. **Oxford Union:** Famous for hosting debates on a wide range of topics, their debates are available on their YouTube channel.

Podcasts:

1. **The Munk Debates Podcast:** Features debates on significant issues, offering insights from various experts.

2. **The Intelligence Squared Podcast:** Provides audio versions of their live debates, suitable for listening on the go.

Social Media:

1. **X:** Follow hashtags related to debates and discussions, such as #Debate or #Discussion, to find live threads and participate in ongoing conversations.

2. **Facebook Groups:** Join groups focused on debate and discussion topics that interest you.

3. TAKE COURSES AND ATTEND WORKSHOPS -

Continuous education in formal settings can provide structure and depth to your learning efforts.

4. **TRAVEL AND CULTURAL IMMERSION** - Experiencing different cultures and environments can dramatically broaden your perspective and inspire new ideas.

If you don't have the time and money to do so, you can also help yourself by watching various travel bloggers on YouTube. Personally, I like these three:

☐ **Kara and Nate**

- Kara and Nate are a couple who have been traveling full-time since 2016, visiting over 100 countries. Their channel features vlogs of their adventures, highlighting unique cultural experiences, local foods, and travel challenges. Their engaging and personal style makes their content both entertaining and informative.

☐ **Mark Wiens**

- Mark Wiens is a food and travel blogger known for his deep dives into local cuisines around the world. His channel focuses on street food, traditional dishes, and the cultural context of the foods he tries. Mark's enthusiasm for food and travel is infectious, making his channel a great resource for cultural immersion through culinary experiences.

☐ **Eva zu Beck**

- Eva zu Beck is a solo traveler and adventure enthusiast who explores off-the-beaten-path destinations around the world. Her channel features immersive travel vlogs, cultural experiences, and personal reflections on travel. Eva's content is both inspiring and educational, offering a unique perspective on global travel and cultural immersion.

By developing a mindset geared towards continuous learning and critical thinking, you not only enhance your understanding of the world but also increase your ability to impact it. As we progress to exploring emotional resilience and independence, it's clear that the intellectually curious are better positioned to manage the complexities of personal and emotional challenges with confidence and insight.

Emotional Resilience and Independence

Emotional resilience and independence are critical faculties that empower people to handle the unpredictable waves of life with grace and strength. These qualities enable one to withstand pressures and adversities without losing inner balance. In this chapter, we assess the essence of emotional resilience, discuss the importance of emotional independence, and offer strategies to improve these powerful attributes.

Emotional resilience is the capacity to recover quickly from difficulties, adjust to change, and persevere through challenges. It involves handling stress, overcoming disappointments, and recovering from failures with a perspective that not only aims to survive but to thrive. This resilience is not an inborn trait but a nurtured skill that grows through experience and deliberate practice.

The core of emotional resilience lies in the way we interpret and respond to challenges. Resilient individuals tend to view difficulties as temporary, isolated, and manageable. They maintain a positive, yet realistic outlook, and see adversities as opportunities for growth and learning. This mindset is crucial because it transforms potential threats into challenges and converts despair into hope.

Emotional independence is the capacity to maintain one's center, make decisions, and function effectively without undue dependence on external validation or emotional support from others. It's about being the master of your emotions, understanding your emotional triggers, and not letting them dictate your actions. This independence is vital for personal development, as it promotes self-confidence and autonomy.

Developing Emotional Resilience and Independence

Here are practical ways to build emotional resilience and promote emotional independence:

1. **Practice Mindfulness and Self-awareness - Mindfulness** meditation and introspective practices help in understanding your emotional patterns and triggers. Awareness is the first step towards control.

At the end of the book, you will find in the designated section a practice that will specifically help you with this.

2. **Develop a Support Network** - While emotional independence is crucial, having a supportive network provides a safety net. Relationships can offer perspectives and feedback that help you grow and adapt.

3. **Set Boundaries** - Learn to say no and set limits. Emotional independence involves respecting your needs and not allowing others to compromise them.

4. **Engage in Reflective Practices** - Keeping a journal, engaging in therapy, or having mentorship can provide insights and facilitate emotional growth. Reflect on experiences to derive lessons and strengthen your emotional understanding.

For this reason, I have written a book specifically on this topic where you will find many exercises of this kind. It's about feminine energy and how to let it blossom, and you can find it by clicking on my author profile. If you've already purchased the bundle, great, I recommend trying the 28-day challenge!

5. **Challenge Yourself Regularly** - Regularly venturing beyond your comfort zone can significantly boost your adaptability and self-confidence. Each challenge overcome is a step towards greater emotional resilience.

These are some activities I can recommend, which for most people, mean stepping out of their comfort zone:

☐ **Public Speaking**

- Join a local Toastmasters club or take a public speaking course to improve your communication skills and gain confidence speaking in front of others.

☐ **Learning a New Language**

- Enroll in a language class or use apps like Duolingo or Rosetta Stone to start learning a language you've always been interested in.

☐ **Physical Challenges**

- Sign up for a marathon, triathlon, or even a local 5k run. Alternatively, try a new sport or join a fitness class like kickboxing, yoga, or rock climbing.

☐ **Traveling Solo**

- Plan a solo trip to a new city or country. Exploring a new environment alone can significantly boost your confidence and independence.

☐ **Taking Up a New Hobby**

- Start a hobby that is completely different from your usual interests, such as painting, dancing, playing a musical instrument, or gardening.

☐ Socializing in New Circles

- Attend social events, networking gatherings, or community meetups where you don't know anyone. This can help you build new connections and improve social skills.

☐Volunteering

- Volunteer for a cause you care about, whether it's at a local shelter, a food bank, or an international volunteer program. This experience can broaden your perspective and provide personal fulfillment.

☐Engaging in Difficult Conversations

- Have a meaningful and honest conversation with someone about a difficult topic or conflict. This can improve your communication skills and emotional intelligence.

Emotional resilience and independence are not just about enduring life's storms; they're about facing them with an empowered, proactive stance. As we explore the power of self-sufficiency in the next section, it's clear that emotional resilience and independence are foundational to living a life of freedom and fulfillment. They enable you to maintain your course even when external circumstances are challenging, ensuring that your sense of self and your path forward are always aligned with your core values and visions.

The Power of Self-Sufficiency

Self-sufficiency is a powerful trait that enables people to rely on their skills and resources to manage life. This quality is about more than just meeting basic needs independently; it's about developing a strong, capable self that thrives in various circumstances, harnessing inner resources to face challenges with confidence and autonomy. In this chapter, we delve into the aspects of self-sufficiency that contribute to a robust, independent lifestyle and how nurturing this trait can lead to a more empowered and fulfilling life.

Self-sufficiency begins with embracing autonomy in all areas of life, from financial independence to decision-making. It involves taking responsibility for your happiness and well-being without relying excessively on external sources. This autonomy is a fundamental aspect of self-empowerment because it places the locus of control within oneself, reducing the impact of external fluctuations on one's emotional and practical stability.

Financial independence is a key component of self-sufficiency. It provides the freedom to make choices that align with personal values and goals without undue influence from external pressures. Developing financial acumen—such as budgeting, saving, and investing—equips individuals with the tools to secure their future and reduce anxiety over economic uncertainties.

Beyond financial independence, self-sufficiency also involves developing a broad set of practical skills that can reduce dependence on others. This includes everyday skills like cooking, basic home repairs, or more advanced capabilities like gardening or DIY projects. Each skill learned not only adds to one's ability to cope with various situations but also boosts confidence and self-reliance.

Moreover, continuous learning and adaptability are crucial in today's fast-paced world. Keeping skills updated and acquiring new knowledge is vital for maintaining self-sufficiency in the professional realm. This ongoing personal development ensures that you remain competitive and capable, no matter how the job market or your circumstances change.

The psychological and emotional benefits of self-sufficiency are profound. Being self-sufficient promotes a sense of competence and efficacy. It builds resilience, as you are more equipped to handle life's challenges without feeling overwhelmed. This resilience, in turn, enhances emotional stability, as you feel less threatened by external changes, knowing you have the capabilities to manage them.

Additionally, self-sufficiency contributes to a healthier state of mind by promoting a proactive rather than reactive approach to life. It encourages setting and achieving personal goals, which is a significant source of intrinsic motivation and satisfaction. Achieving goals based on personal effort and skills reinforces a positive self-image and fosters a sense of purpose.

In conclusion, the power of self-sufficiency lies in its ability to transform not just the practical aspects of life but also the psychological landscape of an individual. By embracing autonomy, developing practical skills, and appreciating the emotional stability it brings, you can enjoy a richer, more independent life. As we have explored the roles of intellectual curiosity, emotional resilience, and now self-sufficiency, it becomes clear that these qualities are interlinked, each reinforcing the others. Together, they form a foundation for a life that is not only self-directed and self-sustained but also deeply fulfilling.

Chapter 8 - The Dark Side of Being a Femme Fatale

In this chapter, we explore the complexities and ethical considerations of embodying the femme fatale archetype. While her allure and strategic acumen are captivating, these traits often come with moral challenges and potential pitfalls. We will examine the use of manipulation and seduction, the resulting isolation and loneliness, and the struggle to maintain personal integrity. Additionally, we will discuss the importance of balancing power with empathy and genuine human connection, highlighting how self-reflection and ethical boundaries can transform her influence into a force for positive, authentic relationships.

Ethical Considerations and Pitfalls of Being a Femme Fatale

The allure of the femme fatale is undeniable. She moves through the world with an enigmatic charm and a strategic mind, often leaving a mark on those she encounters. However, embracing such a powerful archetype comes with its own set of ethical considerations and potential pitfalls. This chapter delves into the moral complexities associated with her persona, exploring the fine line between using one's attributes for personal gain and crossing into morally ambiguous territory.

One of the central ethical concerns surrounding this fatale figure revolves around her use of manipulation and seduction. These tools, while effective in achieving strategic goals, raise significant moral questions. The power to influence can quickly become the power to exploit, leading to situations where the autonomy and dignity of others are compromised. This manipulation, often romanticized in various narratives, needs scrutiny to understand its impact on interpersonal relationships and societal norms.

In considering the ethical implications, it's crucial to evaluate the intentions behind the actions. Is the influence exerted for self-defense or survival, or is it used to assert dominance and control purely for personal gain? The femme fatale often operates in a realm where ethical boundaries are tested, making it vital for any individual who finds resonance with this archetype to consider the consequences of their actions on others' lives.

The moral ambiguity that often accompanies her actions can lead to several pitfalls, notably the risk of self-alienation and the loss of personal integrity. Living in the shadows of ethical grey areas can erode one's sense of self, as the lines between right and wrong blur. This can lead to a disconnection from one's moral compass, with long-term consequences for personal and professional relationships.

Moreover, she may find herself trapped by her persona, pigeonholed into a role that leaves little room for genuine emotional connections or ethical growth. The expectation to continually manipulate situations can become a burden, overshadowing the individual's deeper values and leading to a crisis of identity.

Living on the ethical edge also has practical repercussions. She may face isolation as others grow wary of her reputation for manipulation. Trust becomes difficult to earn, and relationships may be superficial, built on a foundation of intrigue rather than genuine connection. The professional and social networks that are so crucial to personal and career development can become strained, limiting opportunities and support systems.
Additionally, she risks legal and social repercussions if her manipulations lead to actions that breach legal or ethical standards. What starts as a strategic advantage can quickly turn into a significant liability, affecting not just the femme fatale but those around her.

This archetype, though potent and alluring, carries a range of ethical considerations that demand careful handling and deep introspection.

It's essential for those who identify with or portray this archetype to remain vigilant about the ethical dimensions of their actions and to strive for balance in their personal and professional lives.

Acknowledging the potential pitfalls and moral complexities of this persona is crucial in maintaining one's integrity and humanity while wielding influence.

As we explore further the loneliness that can accompany such a lifestyle and the importance of balancing power with humanity, these ethical considerations provide a necessary foundation for understanding the deeper implications of the femme fatale's dark side.

The Loneliness of Manipulation

The persona of the femme fatale, characterized by her adeptness at manipulation and control, often conceals a less visible but profound aspect of her existence—loneliness. This isolation is not merely a byproduct of her actions but a fundamental component of the lifestyle she leads. In this section, we explore how the intrinsic loneliness that accompanies excessive manipulation impacts her interactions and personal experiences.

Manipulation, a tool frequently employed to control her environment, requires a calculated detachment from genuine emotional engagement. To manipulate effectively, one must often suppress or conceal their true feelings, presenting only what is strategically advantageous. This detachment, while useful in achieving immediate goals, creates barriers to authentic connections with others. She may find herself surrounded by people yet fundamentally alone, as her relationships are built on a foundation of deception or calculated interactions rather than mutual trust and respect.

The loneliness is further compounded by the distrust it engenders in others. Those who become aware of her manipulative tendencies may become cautious, keeping her at arm's length. Over time, this wariness can evolve into a pervasive sense of isolation, as she finds that few, if any, are willing to engage with her deeply or openly. This distrust can be a double-edged sword, protecting her from potential threats but also depriving her of the chance to experience genuine human connections.

Internally, she might struggle with her perceptions of self-worth and identity. If her manipulative behaviors are not just roles she plays but become integral to her identity, she may begin to question her authenticity. Who is she beneath these facades? Does she manipulate because she chooses to, or because she feels there is no other way to maintain control and power? This existential questioning can intensify feelings of loneliness, as she grapples with these internal conflicts in isolation, without the support of a trusted confidante.

While she may enjoy temporary advantages through manipulation, such as gaining power or achieving specific goals, these victories often come with an emotional cost. The paradox lies in her ability to influence others so effectively while being unable to form the emotional bonds that humans inherently need for psychological well-being. This lack of genuine emotional exchange can lead to a hollow existence, filled with accomplishments but devoid of meaningful emotional satisfaction.

It is important to note that manipulation does not automatically lead to loneliness. This outcome arises primarily when manipulation is used excessively or improperly. When used sparingly and with consideration, manipulation can be a strategic tool without necessarily isolating the individual.

The loneliness stemming from reliance on manipulation serves as a poignant reminder of the human need for genuine relationships and trust. This section not only illuminates the personal costs associated with such a lifestyle but also underscores the importance of introspection and change. Understanding the depths of this loneliness presents an opportunity for her to reconsider her path and seek a balance that allows for both personal empowerment and emotional fulfillment. As we continue to explore how she might balance her power with her humanity, we can appreciate the complex nature of her persona and the potential for growth beyond the constraints of her archetype.

Balancing Power with Humanity

The charm of the femme fatale often stems from her remarkable ability to wield power and influence. However, maintaining this power without losing touch with one's humanity presents a profound challenge. This section analyzes how she can manage the delicate balance between exercising control and retaining essential human qualities such as empathy, kindness, and genuine connection.

One key strategy is to embrace empathy. Understanding and sharing the feelings of others can seem antithetical to the manipulative traits typically associated with her character. However, integrating empathy into her interactions allows for deeper, more meaningful connections. Transforming relationships from tools of manipulation to genuine engagements enriches her understanding of others, enhancing her influence by grounding it in authenticity rather than deceit.

Integrity, the quality of being honest and having strong moral principles, is also crucial. Maintaining integrity means aligning actions with ethical standards that respect the dignity of others while pursuing goals. This might involve setting clear boundaries on acceptable behavior to ensure that the pursuit of power does not lead to harm or injustice. Adhering to a code of integrity allows her to hold onto power without compromising her moral core, establishing respect not just for her cunning but for her character.

To counterbalance the loneliness and isolation that often accompany manipulative behavior, she can focus on nurturing genuine relationships based on mutual trust and respect. These relationships, built on transparency and sincerity, provide emotional and psychological support. They serve as a reminder that her worth extends beyond the ability to manipulate and control, residing also in the capacity to love, support, and contribute positively to others' lives.

A critical component of balancing power with humanity is ongoing self-reflection. Regularly assessing motivations and the impact of actions is essential. She must ask herself whether she is acting out of a desire for control or from a deeper, more holistic understanding of her goals. Self-reflection enables recognition of veering towards unethical behavior and realigning actions with values. It also promotes personal growth, encouraging evolution beyond the limited identity of a manipulator to a more rounded, introspective individual.

Balancing power with humanity allows her to wield influence more wisely and sustainably. By integrating empathy, maintaining integrity, nurturing genuine relationships, and engaging in self-reflection, she can manage the complex interplay between power and vulnerability. This balance not only enhances effectiveness but also enriches life, providing a path to fulfillment that honors both ambitions and humanity. Exploring the intricate dynamics of this balance reveals a path forward that respects power and profound connection to the human experience, demonstrating that true strength lies in the harmony of power and compassion.

Chapter 9 – Real Life Femme Fatales

Throughout history, numerous women have exemplified the qualities of the femme fatale, using their intelligence, charm, and strategic skills to influence the events and people around them. This chapter highlights several notable historical figures who have embodied this archetype, exploring their backgrounds and the contexts that shaped their legendary reputations. From Cleopatra VII's political alliances to Ching Shih's command over a vast pirate fleet, we will examine how these women used their unique positions and skills to leave an indelible mark on history. Their stories offer valuable insights into the dynamics of power and influence, showcasing the interplay between personal ambition and societal structures. As we analyze their lives and strategies, we will uncover lessons that remain relevant today, illustrating the timeless nature of these remarkable women's impact.

Historical Examples of Real-Life Femme Fatales

Throughout history, numerous women have embodied the femme fatale archetype, maneuvering through their environments with cunning, charm, and strategic acumen. These women, often positioned at pivotal moments in history, utilized their intelligence and allure not just to survive but to exert significant influence on the events and figures around them. This subchapter explores several historical examples of real-life femme fatales, delving into their backgrounds and the contexts that shaped their legendary reputations.

Cleopatra VII of Egypt

Cleopatra VII, the last pharaoh of Ptolemaic Egypt, famously used her intelligence, political savvy, and personal charm to forge alliances with Rome's most powerful leaders, Julius Caesar and Mark Antony. Her strategic romantic and political alliances were aimed at securing her throne and preserving Egypt's independence in the face of the expanding Roman Empire.

Ching Shih

Ching Shih, originally a prostitute, rose to become one of the most powerful and successful pirates in history. After marrying a notorious pirate, she took over his fleet after his death, commanding over 300 ships and 40,000 pirates. Her leadership was marked by rigorous discipline, tactical prowess, and shrewd negotiations with the Chinese government, which eventually allowed her to retire with her wealth and amnesty.

Anne Bonny

Anne Bonny was an infamous pirate operating in the Caribbean during the early 18th century. Known for her fiery temper and fearsome disposition, Anne defied the conventional expectations of women by dressing as a man and fighting alongside her crew. She partnered with Calico Jack Rackham and Mary Read in piratical ventures, becoming a legendary figure in pirate lore. Her life story is filled with tales of daring, combat, and survival against the odds.

Lola Montez

Lola Montez was an Irish dancer and actress who became famous as a courtesan and the mistress of King Ludwig I of Bavaria. Her influence was so profound that it is credited with contributing to the king's abdication. Known for her beauty and clever manipulation of her image and identity, Montez crafted a persona that allowed her to ascend socially and politically, wielding considerable influence in Bavarian court politics.

These historical figures demonstrate the multifaceted nature of the femme fatale archetype in real life. They steer through complex social and political landscapes, using their intelligence, charisma, and, where necessary, seductive prowess to influence and manipulate events and people to their advantage. Each of these women, from rulers and pirates to dancers and courtesans, utilized their unique positions and skills to craft legacies that still captivate and provoke debate today. As we move into analyzing their lives and strategies, we can draw lessons from their experiences, applying these insights to understand better the dynamics of power and influence.

Analysis of Their Lives and Strategies

The lives of historical femme fatales provide rich case studies in the art of strategy and influence. Each woman, uniquely positioned within her specific cultural and historical context, leveraged her intelligence and personal charm to maneuver and manipulate power structures. This analysis explores the key strategies employed by these femme fatales, revealing how their actions reflect broader themes of resilience, adaptability, and the quest for autonomy.

Cleopatra VII of Egypt: Diplomacy and Alliances

Cleopatra's strategic acumen was evident in her use of diplomacy and personal alliances to bolster Egypt's position against Rome. Understanding the political landscape of the time, Cleopatra sought alliances that would strengthen her rule and secure her nation's future. Her relationships with Julius Caesar and later Mark Antony were not just romantic entanglements but calculated political moves designed to forge a bond between Egypt and Rome, the superpower of the era. Cleopatra's ability to engage with some of the most powerful men of her time and influence Roman politics was a testament to her intelligence and diplomatic prowess.

Ching Shih: Command and Governance

Ching Shih's strategy centered on strict governance and the establishment of a code of laws within her pirate confederation. Her leadership style was authoritarian yet effective, keeping thousands of pirates under control with a strict set of rules that regulated everything from division of loot to treatment of prisoners. This rigid structure not only minimized internal conflicts but also maximized operational efficiency, allowing her fleet to become a formidable force in the South China Sea. Her negotiation of amnesty from the Chinese government, which allowed her and her followers to retire without punishment, showcased her skill in leveraging her power for a secure and peaceful retirement.

Anne Bonny: Rebellion and Identity

Anne Bonny's life was a continuous defiance of the societal norms that restricted women's roles in the 18th century. By dressing as a man and participating in piracy, she not only challenged these norms but also crafted an identity that gave her access to opportunities otherwise denied to women of her time. Her strategy was one of outright rebellion; by stepping into a male-dominated world, she gained freedom and a measure of respect that would have been impossible in conventional roles. Her fearless engagement in battles and raids made her a respected figure among pirates, proving that her tactical mind and combat skills were as sharp as any of her male counterparts.

Lola Montez: Manipulation and Image Crafting

Lola Montez's strategy was built around her ability to manipulate her image and background to ascend through social ranks. By reinventing herself—from her name to her history—Lola crafted a mysterious and alluring persona that captivated those around her, including King Ludwig I of Bavaria. Her influence over Ludwig, driven by her charismatic presence and bold personality, led to significant political sway within the Bavarian court. However, her story also highlights the risks involved in such strategies, as her fall from grace was swift once her true background was discovered and political tides turned against her.

These women exemplified the femme fatale's ability to manage and manipulate their environments through a combination of strategic alliances, command over followers, rebellion against societal expectations, and masterful image crafting. Their lives remind us of the power of personal agency and the complex interplay between individual ambitions and the broader social and political contexts. As we reflect on these strategies, we gain insights into not only their successes but also the challenges and consequences they faced, providing valuable lessons on the dynamics of power and influence.

Lessons Learned from Their Experiences

The experiences of historical femme fatales offer rich insights into the complexities of power dynamics, personal ambition, and societal limitations. Reflecting on their lives allows us to extract meaningful and applicable lessons not only in understanding history but also in navigating contemporary challenges. Here, we explore the key lessons that can be learned from the strategic lives of these remarkable women.

The Importance of Strategic Relationships

From Cleopatra's alliances with Rome's most powerful leaders to Lola Montez's influential relationship with King Ludwig I, the importance of strategic relationships is a recurring theme in the lives of femme fatales. These relationships were not mere liaisons but carefully calculated moves to gain and maintain power. The lesson here is clear: understanding and leveraging the dynamics of relationships can significantly alter one's position within any power structure. It teaches us the value of alliances and partnerships in achieving one's goals, whether in business, politics, or personal endeavors.

Handling Power with Agility

Ching Shih's governance of her pirate fleet and Anne Bonny's defiance of gender roles exemplify the adaptability required to steer and maintain power in challenging environments. Both women adapted to their circumstances with incredible foresight and flexibility, which was crucial to their survival and success. This underscores the importance of adaptability and resilience in leadership and life. Being open to change and prepared to pivot strategies in response to new challenges is essential for sustaining success and influence.

The Risks and Rewards of Defying Norms

Anne Bonny and Lola Montez both lived lives that starkly defied the societal norms of their times. Their stories teach us about the double-edged sword of such defiance. While breaking from tradition can lead to unprecedented freedom and opportunities, it can also result in significant social backlash and personal risk. The key takeaway is to weigh the risks and rewards of challenging established norms and to be prepared for the potential consequences of such actions.

The Power of Personal Branding

Lola Montez's manipulation of her image and background highlights the power of personal branding. Her ability to craft and control her persona allowed her to maneuver through social hierarchies and influence high-ranking people. This lesson is particularly relevant in today's digital age, where personal branding has become a crucial component of professional and personal success. Understanding how to effectively present oneself can open doors and create opportunities in almost any sphere.

Ethical Considerations and Long-term Consequences

Reflecting on the ethical implications of the femme fatales' strategies offers a cautionary perspective on the use of manipulation and deceit. While these tactics can provide short-term gains, they often lead to long-term consequences that can damage reputations and relationships. This teaches us the importance of considering the ethical dimensions of our actions and their potential impact on our long-term personal and professional lives.

The historical femme fatales teach us about the complexity of managing power and influence within restrictive societal structures. Their lives offer lessons on strategic thinking, adaptability, the importance of relationships, and the careful management of one's image.

By studying their stories, we can glean insights into effective strategies for handling challenges, the importance of ethical considerations, and the impact of our choices on our broader social and personal outcomes. These lessons are timeless and continue to resonate, guiding anyone looking to understand the dynamics of power and influence in any context.

Introduction to Positive Affirmations for Becoming a Femme Fatale

PART OPTIMIZED FOR THE AUDIO VERSION

In this chapter, I will share with you the transformative power of positive affirmations, specifically curated to help you embody the essence of a femme fatale. Positive affirmations are potent tools for reshaping your mindset, boosting self-confidence, and enhancing various aspects of your persona.

By consistently listening to and repeating these affirmations, you can develop confidence and poise, refine your style, improve your emotional intelligence, and amplify your natural allure and seductive charm.

Positive affirmations work by reinforcing positive thoughts and beliefs, gradually replacing any negative or self-limiting patterns. They help to rewire your subconscious mind, paving the way for lasting changes in your attitude and behavior.

When you regularly engage with these affirmations, you begin to internalize these empowering statements, making them a natural part of your self-perception and daily life.

For optimal results, I recommend you to listen and repeat these affirmations at specific times of the day when your mind is most receptive.

Ideally, start your day by listening to these affirmations in the morning, allowing their positive energy to set the tone for your day. You can also integrate them into your evening routine, helping to reinforce these positive beliefs as you unwind and prepare for rest.

Consistency is key, so aim to engage with these affirmations at least 10mins daily to begin noticing significant shifts in your mindset and self-confidence.

As you begin this journey of self-transformation, remember that becoming a femme fatale is not just about outward appearances; it's about embodying an inner strength, grace, and allure that radiates from within. Let these positive affirmations guide and inspire you as you unlock your full potential and embrace the captivating, confident woman you are meant to be.

Important: I have left a pause between each positive affirmation to give you time to repeat it. In addition to listening, repeating it is essential to amplify their effectiveness.

Positive affirmations about confidence and poise

1. I am confident in my abilities.
2. I exude poise and grace in all situations.
3. I trust myself and my instincts.
4. I handle challenges with calm and confidence.
5. I believe in my potential to succeed.
6. I am proud of who I am and who I am becoming.
7. I face every day with confidence and a positive attitude.
8. I speak clearly and confidently.
9. I am composed and centered in all situations.
10. My confidence grows with every step I take.
11. I am capable and strong.
12. I embrace opportunities with confidence and enthusiasm.
13. I am a powerful.
14. I radiate confidence and positivity.
15. I handle stress with poise and calm.
16. I trust myself to make the right decisions.
17. I am in control of my emotions and reactions.
18. I am assertive and stand up for myself.
19. I am at peace with who I am.

[This was just a part of the positive affirmations.
Since it is optimized for the audio version, the complete chapter with all the most effective positive affirmations about confidence and poise is available in the audio version.]

Introduction to Visualization Exercises for Style and Attractiveness

PART OPTIMIZED FOR THE AUDIO VERSION

In this chapter, we explore the transformative practice of visualization exercises, specifically designed to enhance your style and elevate your seductive allure.

Visualization is a powerful technique that leverages the mind's ability to create vivid mental images, helping you to embody the qualities and confidence of a true femme fatale. By regularly engaging in these exercises, you can develop a more refined sense of style and amplify your natural attractiveness.

Visualization works by tapping into the subconscious mind, which does not distinguish between real and imagined experiences. By vividly picturing yourself exuding confidence, style, and allure, you effectively train your mind to adopt these attributes in real life.

Over time, these mental rehearsals can lead to tangible changes in your behavior, posture, and overall presence.

For the best results, practice these visualization exercises in a quiet, relaxed environment where you can fully concentrate.

Morning and evening are ideal times to engage in these exercises, as your mind is generally more receptive and less cluttered with daily distractions. Aim to do at least one visualization session per day, allowing yourself to fully immerse in the visualizations.

Guided Visualization: Developing Style and Elegance

PART OPTIMIZED FOR THE AUDIO VERSION

Find a quiet place where you can sit or lie down comfortably, ensuring you will not be disturbed. Begin to relax by taking a deep breath in through your nose, holding it for a moment, and then slowly exhaling through your mouth. Repeat this breathing exercise several times until you feel calm and centered.

Now, with your eyes closed, imagine yourself completely relaxed, with no tension in your body. You can start from your head and gradually move down to your feet, relaxing each muscle along the way.

Now that you are completely relaxed, let's set the intention for this visualization session. Our goal is to develop a strong sense of style and elegance in both dress and movement. Keep this intention in mind as we proceed with the visualization.

Imagine yourself in a bright and spacious room, with a large wardrobe in front of you. This is no ordinary wardrobe; it is a magical place filled with the most elegant and suitable clothing for you. Each piece has been carefully selected to express your personality and highlight your best features.

[This was just a part of the guided visualization session. Being a part optimized for the audio version, the complete chapter is available in the audio version.]

Conclusion – Adopting your Inner Femme Fatale

Integrating Femme Fatale Qualities into Everyday Life

Adopting the qualities of the femme fatale archetype isn't about adopting a persona of manipulation or danger; rather, it's about tapping into a profound sense of empowerment, self-awareness, and strategic acumen. By integrating these traits, you can enrich their personal and professional lives, maneuvering challenges with grace and fortitude. This chapter explores practical ways to embody her strengths in everyday situations, encouraging a balance of assertiveness, emotional intelligence, and authentic self-expression.

One of the key attributes of this powerful persona is a strategic approach to life's challenges. You can develop this in your own life by planning with foresight and intentionality. Begin by setting clear, actionable goals for both the short-term and the long-term. Approach these goals with a mindset of flexibility and adaptability, recognizing that circumstances may change and require you to adjust your strategies accordingly. This kind of strategic planning isn't just about achieving objectives but about understanding the bigger picture and how your actions fit within it.

The ability to handle complex social dynamics is grounded in high emotional intelligence. Enhancing your EI can transform your interpersonal relationships and self-perception. Start by becoming more attuned to your emotions and the emotions of others. Practice active listening and empathy in your daily interactions, and actively solicit feedback to gain insight into how others view you. By managing your emotions and responding effectively to those around you, you can build stronger, more meaningful connections.

Embodying assertiveness means speaking up for yourself and your needs while respecting the rights and opinions of others. Develop your confidence by taking on challenges that push you out of your comfort zone, and celebrate your successes, no matter how small. Confidence comes from a series of achievements and the recognition of your capabilities. Remember, assertiveness is about being clear and direct in your communication, not about being aggressive.

Just as this archetype carefully curates her appearance and demeanor to suit her purposes, you too can harness the power of self-presentation. This doesn't mean changing who you are but rather being mindful of how you present yourself in different contexts. Consider how your appearance, body language, and speech patterns can influence people's perceptions and the outcomes of your interactions. Dressing appropriately and using confident, open body language can significantly affect how you are perceived and, consequently, how you feel about yourself.

Finally, integrate resilience into your life. Life is full of unexpected twists and turns, and resilience is about bouncing back from setbacks with even greater resolve. Promote resilience by maintaining a positive outlook, setting realistic expectations, and viewing failures as opportunities to learn and grow. Adaptability goes hand in hand with resilience; being flexible in your approach allows you to face life's uncertainties more smoothly.

Integrating these qualities into your daily life is about embracing a powerful blend of mindfulness, strategy, and authenticity. These traits are not reserved for fictional characters or historical figures; they are accessible to anyone willing to develop them.

By adopting these qualities, you can enhance your empowerment and steer your life's journey with confidence and poise. As we explore further in the next chapters, remember that the journey of self-discovery and empowerment is continuous, filled with opportunities to learn and grow. Embrace these opportunities, and let this archetype inspire you to live your life with boldness and elegance.

Encouragements for Continued Growth

As you integrate these aspects of the femme fatale archetype into your daily life, remember that this is a journey of continuous improvement and self-discovery. Be patient with yourself as you experiment with these techniques, and don't hesitate to adjust your approach based on what feels most authentic to you. The goal is not to transform into someone else but to find ways to express your unique self with more confidence and clarity.

Incorporating these qualities is about more than adopting certain postures or gestures; it's about integrating an entire communicative repertoire that enhances your interactions and deepens your connections. These skills empower you to present yourself as both approachable and authoritative, mirroring the complex allure of the femme fatale while maintaining your authenticity. As you practice and embody these principles, you'll find that they not only improve how others perceive you but also how you perceive yourself—stronger, more confident, and ready to engage the world on your terms.

Remember, this journey is filled with opportunities to learn and grow. Embrace these opportunities, and let the archetype inspire you to live your life with boldness and elegance.

www.ingramcontent.com/pod-product-compliance
Lightning Source LLC
Chambersburg PA
CBHW061048250726
48653CB00001B/300